The Shrinking Sands of an African American Beach

Acclaim for *The Shrinking Sands of an African American Beach*

"Your revelation of historic findings, documentations and true life experiences in your determination to retain this valuable asset, American Beach and its environs, is surely deserving of being treasured for posterity. Those who like yourself might have even a single iota of additional knowledge ought seek to join your noble effort in broadening this horizon of truth. We must be ever mindful that it is only through the unrelenting quest of stalwart warriors that victories are won.

We salute you in your struggle.

We, the Board of the Virginia Key Beach Park Trust of Miami-Dade County, struggle on a similar battlefield to retain Virginia Key Beach Park, which is rightfully ours; having been acquired under the mantle of appeasement toward our black citizenry, who for numberless years were denied the use of any public beach in Dade County under the law of segregation of the races.

We, too, will be stalwart warriors to restore the past, improve the present and build for the future.

It is our ultimate goal to erect an historical museum at Virginia Key Beach Park wherein generations yet unborn will be privileged to learn of our battles fought and our victories won."

M. Athalie Range
Former Commissioner, City of Miami
Former Secretary of Community Affairs, State of Florida
Former Chair of the Virginia Key Beach Park Trust
Mrs. Range wrote the comments above on the first edition of The Shrinking Sands in 2006. She is now deceased.

"Written to highlight the preservation of Florida's historic resources, *The Shrinking Sands* documents the struggles of an historic seaside community to keep its sense of identity. Historic preservation is an important topic that should always be at the forefront of any conversation regarding future development."

Phyllis Davis
Executive Director
Amelia Island Museum of History

The Shrinking Sands of an
African American Beach

ANNETTE McCOLLOUGH MYERS

Second Edition, Revised and Expanded

Library of Congress Control Number: 2005932010

Myers, Annette McCollough
The Shrinking Sands of an African American Beach

ISBN-13 978-1-934666-78-4

1st Edition 2006 by Lexington Ventures, Inc.
2nd Edition 2011 by High-Pitched Hum Publishing

High-Pitched Hum Publishing
321 15th Street North
Jacksonville Beach, Florida 32250

Contact High-Pitched Hum Publishing at www.highpitchedhum.net

99 98 97 96 95 5 4 3 2 1
First Paperback Edition

Cover: The author is pictured amongst the dunes in the community she
so dearly loves and, with others, has attempted to preserve.

Front Cover Photo by James Robinson
Book Layout by Jennifer Wehrmann

High-Pitched Hum
Publishing

Dedication

This book is dedicated to my father, Wendell Herbert McCollough, also known as W. H. or Captain Mac, who passed away March 19, 1993, and to my mother, Janie Lang McCollough, who maintained control of the family until her demise January 8, 2006.

To my deceased husband of thirty years, Elmo Vincent Myers, also known as E.V. Myers, who passed away March 28, 1987.

To our son, Donald Myers, and his wife, who by inheritance and in the course of time may contribute to the American Beach legacy.

To my in-laws, Jim and Muriel Williams, and Elmo H. Myers, for they are somewhere around God's throne.

To all my nieces, nephews, other relatives, and my friends, that they will learn more about American Beach and may soon, in some way and somehow, become investors before it is too late.

A 1930s cast iron license plate topper that reads "AMERICAN BEACH FLA. NEGRO OCEAN PLAYGROUND."

Contents

Sherald Wilson - July 2005

Historic American Beach Marker. The historic marker was approved by the Florida Department of State, ordered November 1999, and erected by the Nassau County Public Works Department. The marker was unveiled and dedicated at the 65th anniversary of American Beach, May 20, 2000.

Preface

HISTORIC AMERICAN BEACH

American Beach was established in 1935 under the leadership of Abraham Lincoln Lewis, one of the seven co-founders of the Afro-American Life Insurance Company, and one of Florida's first black millionaires. His vision was to create a beach resort as a benefit for company executives and as an incentive for employees to exceed in sales. Florida's beaches were racially segregated until the passage of the 1964 Civil Rights Act. Because of this, American Beach became regionally popular since it was one of the few beaches in the Southeast open to African-Americans. Other sites on American Beach trace their history to the Civil War era. Amelia Island was home to several Sea Island cotton plantations, including the Harrison Plantation. In 1862, Union Forces captured Amelia Island and the freed slaves founded Franklin Town at the south end of this island. The Franklin Town Cemetery, which had been given by the Harrison family to their slaves as a burial place for their families, still exists today on the west side of Highway AIA. In 1972, encroaching development forced Franklin Town residents to move north to American Beach. Their Methodist Church, built in 1949, was also moved here where it now serves as the church's fellowship hall.

FLORIDA HERITAGE LANDMARK
SPONSORED BY THE
AMERICAN BEACH PROPERTY OWNERS' ASSOCIATION, INC.
F-417   AND THE FLORIDA DEPARTMENT OF STATE   1999

This book is not to appease or diminish anyone, but to state the facts as they occurred in the course of time.

I have attempted to address the struggles of a 70-plus-year-old seaside community, inhabited by African-Americans, that according to predictions would be non-existent today and swallowed up by developers. Quite the contrary!

American Beach, located on Amelia Island, Nassau County, Florida, is now boxed in by upscale resorts and residential neighborhoods, and to the east by the Atlantic Ocean.

American Beach accomplished its first landmark and earned its place in history in 1990, when the Study Commission on African-American History was formed by the Florida Legislature in Tallahassee to discuss a list of sites for possible inclusion on the Black Heritage Trail. In its publication by the Department of State, American Beach is listed as the northernmost and first site of 141 sites in the Sunshine State of Florida.

Over the past several years, my writings have consisted of quite a few newspaper articles on various topics and subjects including American Beach, but nothing this extensive about the community I live in. Since returning to American Beach(1967), my participation in community affairs have continuously escalated. I have acted in the capacity of vice president (1991) and president of the American Beach Property Owners' Association (1992-2001). I successfully carried out the effort by the association and the tremendous amount of paperwork and documenration required to place American Beach on the National Register of Historic Places. Originally chartered in 1982, I led the reorganization of the association and revamping of its charter in 1996. In March of 2005, I decided to share my flight in time by telling my part of the story from my personal archives and experiences.

The marker story on the previous page, which was cited under my administration as president, has been told over and over and time and time again. Regardless of what the future holds for American Beach, it is my desire that this story will continue to be told for generations to come.

American Beach has a rich heritage and legacy as it represents the ties that bind. Much more is yet to be told as the community continues to age and again, hopefully, prosper.

Acknowledgements

I wish to thank the American Beach community during my years of service as president and vice president. The ups and downs, the pros and cons helped to strengthen me as agent, community representative, and spokesperson. Thanks to all the news media coverage over the years for telling it like it is, the special stories and editions, about me, of the *Amelia Islander Magazine* of April 2002, and the *Florida Trend Magazine* of June 1999; to Dr. Nettie Cook Dove, now deceased, my high school science teacher, for her special framing of Martha Hippard's Hideaway; James and Joyce Robinson for their hand crafted wood plaque of seashells and news clippings; Antonio Carey, my nephew, for helping me develop the Miss Martha's Hideaway website; my church—the New Zion Missionary Baptist Church membership who on the spot hosted my National Register Celebration in the church auditorium due to inclement weather—Rev. Jeremiah Robinson, Jr., pastor; Rev. Marcelle Myers and the Myers family for their assistance anytime I call on them.

Thanks to the relatives and wife Florence Mayer of the Frank Mayer family, the Frank Johnson relatives, the Birdie Delaney relatives, and the relatives of Lottie O. Harris.

Special acknowledgements to Don Shaw, former owner of Books Plus, and author Jan H. Johannes, Sr., for their generous help and direction, and James Robinson, my neighbor, who took many of the pictures in my personal files. I never knew why I took interest in having so many pictures, but now I know why.

I cherish the ability to write and the opportunity given me since August of 2000 as a journalist by publisher and managing editor Darryl A. Barrs, Sr. of the *Christian Reader "Good News"* newspaper of Daytona Beach, Florida.

All these experiences and relationships, plus others I may not have mentioned, played an important part to me in developing this book and allowing me to leave my footprints on the sands of time at an African-American Beach.My thanks and appreciation to my sister, Dr. Barbara M. Carey-Shuler, for proofreading and editing the first few drafts of my manuscript.

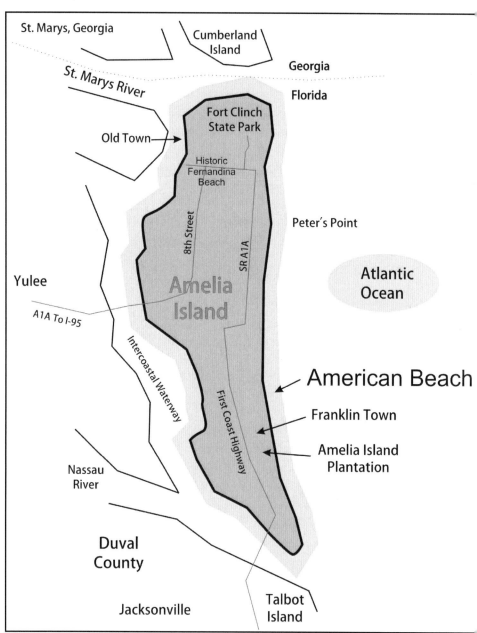

In late 2010, Amelia Island Plantation (AIP), under new ownership, was renamed the Omni Amelia Island Plantation.

Illustrated by Jan Johannes

"The Shrinking Sands of an African American Beach is not a story of the founding of American Beach . . .Instead it offers a perspective on what has happened in the middle phase of American Beach's evolution into what it is today."—Mary Hurst, "American Beach Story–written by a resident," *Florida Times-Union/Nassau Neighbors,* September 2006.

Introduction

The ultimate purpose of this book is to document, as much as possible, the historical milestones of the struggles and changing times of this unique and long-standing American Beach community.

Where many significant historic communities have disappeared or fallen apart, this expanded second edition of *Shrinking Sands* includes additional chapters and pertinent information to capture the ongoing events and continuation of historic American Beach in this 21st century.

"If a man owns land, the land owns him."
(Ralph Waldo Emerson - Wealth*)*

Chapter 1

Summertime Fun - Shut out by Jim Crow, but at Home in Our Own World.

WEEKDAYS AT THE BEACH

My early days of sand, sun, and surf at American Beach came as a child when parents or neighbors in the community, or church members got together to take the children on picnics to the beach. We rode on the back of big trucks used for hauling large loads, owned by men of the community. I remember the trucks were so big, the adults sat in chairs in the back of the trucks.

American Beach was not considered historic at that time. We just knew we had our own little mecca Easter Sunday to Labor Day, and from sun up to sun down. This was the official beach season and "The Beach" was "the place" for black people to go, to be in our own world, to play ball, and to enjoy the sand and surf. A trip to the beach was always fun and scary for me, too, while traveling on the back of a loaded truck down the rut-ridden Lewis Street dirt road. I often thought we would get stuck and have to get out and push the truck with all the ruts in the roadway. Luckily, we never did. Lewis Street was not Lewis Street without getting a drink of sulfur water from the ever-flowing artesian well that was always there in the first block on the left of the roadway. The rotten eggshell smelling water was so good and thirst quenching. Later, Lewis Street, which I knew as the <u>Beach Road</u>, became a shell road. Then on to the pavilion to change into a bathing suit if you did not already have it on, and after

My friend and high school classmate, Liz (now Dr. Liz Jordan), from St. Marys, Georgia. The picture was taken inside the photo booth at El-Patio on American Beach. Liz played cupid between me and her homeboy E.V. Myers, also of St. Marys. July 4, 1953.

Annette McCollough and Elmo V. (E.V.) Myers in 1955, the year I graduated from Peck High School in Fernandina and entered Florida A. and M. University in Tallahassee, Florida. We visited the beach and dined at Williams Guest Lodge. We were married June 16, 1956, in Camden County Georgia.

My sister-in-law, Gwendolyn Myers, and me at the beach. The picture was taken in the photo booth at El-Patio in the summer of 1956.

Maggie Carey - 1963

My mother, father, and their oldest grandson, Wendell, enjoying a day at the beach in 1963.

coming out of the water to shower at the pavilion and change into dry clothes. That was followed by packed picnic lunches and drinks prepared by the adults for everyone to enjoy.

SUNDAY AFTERNOONS AT THE BEACH

Sunday afternoons at the beach were different, when hundreds and hundreds of visitors from everywhere found the intersection of Lewis and Gregg Streets, and the big parking lot, an exciting place to be. There you would find people wearing bathing suit fashions of all kinds, automobiles of all kinds, alcohol and food aromas of all kinds, and people just having a partying good time. Located at the dead end of Lewis Street, and near by, were popular places and restaurants. These businesses originated and accommodated the visitors.

There was a place near the beach walkover called Sweet Tooth where great smelling cotton candy was sold. There was El-Patio, for food, dancing, soft drinks, beer, and a photo booth. There was Reynold's Sandwich Shop next door to El-Patio. Williams Guest Lodge was located at the north end of Gregg Street. My husband and I would go there often where we could reminisce and get a tasty seafood dinner with waitress style service, personally served by the owners we knew so well.

Duck's Ocean Vu-Inn on Lewis Street between Ervin and James Streets was much like Williams Guest Lodge where you could take your special friends to a delicious sit-down dinner. I remember going there with people like the President of Florida A. and M. University, George W. Gore and his wife, and eating there with my mother and other guests. Dr. Gore was my undergraduate alma mater president who was, at that time, vacationing at the famous A.L. (Abraham Lincoln) Lewis Motel on Gregg Street. Evans' Rendezvous, sometimes called the liquor store, was known for mouth-watering barbeque and seafood, drinks, beer, liquor, and a patio outside facing the ocean. The Rendezvous was quite a place where social clubs and other groups often scheduled special events during other days of the week, excluding Sundays. On Sunday afternoons, there would be so many people, you had to edge your way to get through the sit-down and stand-up crowds. Then, there was Dad and Chicks down the street south of the Rendezvous known for good food, soft drinks, and beer. We also claimed the Honey Dripper out on A1A. The beach was not "The Beach" without the Honey Dripper because this establishment had a bar and sold liquor just like the Rendezvous. Back in those times, it was a big thing if you were a black business and could own a liquor license. Also, no one looked at you funny for being at the Honey Dripper for good food, fun, and listening to the "juke box" blasting away the popular oldies of the 50s and 60s. Even those "old" sanctimonious folks would be poppin' in and out. Crowds that were not already at the Honey Dripper headed there when it got dark at the entertainment area around Lewis and Gregg Streets.

Those were the good ole' days, and this was our land! We were shut out of the white world by Jim Crow laws, but we were at home and felt safe and protected in our own world.

Photo by the Author - 2006

As it looked in 2006, the famous Honey Dripper, another historical landmark, which was torn down in 2007 to make room for luxury townhouses.[1]

"The reason why men enter into society is the
preservation of their property."
(John Locke, 1632-1704)

Chapter 2

American Beach Since the 1960s

In the 1960s, when American Beach began to lose its prominence due
to the destruction of Hurricane Dora and integration, property owners along with community citizens and anyone else concerned about
the welfare of American Beach formed *American Beach, Incorporated*, a
non-profit organization with Ben Durham serving as president and
registered agent. The charter was filed February 26, 1982, with the
late Elmo Myers and I as founding members.[1] The main purpose was
revitalization, improvement, perpetuation, and upkeep of this African-
American coastal community.

Although not attracting the kinds of visitors including family
oriented groups it once had, American Beach still drew large crowds
on Sundays causing parking problems and law enforcement problems.
This resulted in several clashes between property owners and beachgoers, as well as between the beachgoers and the Nassau County
Sheriff's Department.

In an attempt to address the various issues and other problems
of parking and beach access, the Nassau County Commissioners, the
Amelia Island Company, and the Plantation Park Development came
together to establish a six-acre beachfront park just south of American
Beach named Burney Park that opened in 1990. The land was donated
to the county by the Amelia Island Plantation (AIP), along with a
$150,000 cash donation, and an easement for water hook-up granted
by the Plantation Homeowners' Association.[2] The park was named in
honor of Isadore Burney II, who owned property at the beach, and
served as president of the Afro-American Life Insurance Company

from 1967 until 1975.[3] Burney Road, the last road on the south end of American Beach, that runs from State Road AIA eastward to Burney Park also carries his name.

American Beach, Inc., later known as the American Beach Property Owners' Association, Incorporated, was constantly confronted with addressing the Sunday afternoon crowd problems, along with other community concerns.

Although the problems did not go away, the beach community began to make improvements. Beach clean-ups began to take place. Some dilapidated and unsafe buildings, over time, were torn down and removed. Other structures, in later years, due to absentee property owners and neglect, eventually became eyesores in the community.

Over several administrations and as time moved on, the organization and meetings were becoming composed of non-property owners and visiting outsiders having more of a say about our investments. There were those who had their own personal agendas and what they wanted American Beach to become, regardless of preserving the historical character of the community.

James Robinson - 1998

The Burney Park entrance sign, and the east end of Burney Road going towards the Burney Park boardwalk beach access.

James Robinson - August 1997

Burney Park from the sand dune inside Burney Park. The south end of American Beach in the background along Gregg Street can be seen from the park.

The parking area of Burney Park.

James Robinson - August 1997

"What our generation has forgotten is that the system of private property is the most important guaranty of freedom, not only for those who own property, but scarcely less for those who do not."

(Friedrich Hayek)

Chapter 3

The American Beach Property Owners' Association, Incorporated (ABPOA, Inc.)

Annette Myers, Vice-President - 1991
President - 1992 to January 2001

Never did I envision from my early days at the beach, that some fifty years later, I would become spokesperson, chief executive officer (CEO), and agent of the community's most prominent, looked upon, and sought out association forum. My name and comments have appeared, sometimes unknown to me, in numerous newspapers and magazines across the United States about American Beach, and at times, after talking with someone I did not realize was the news media.

April 16, 1996, through council attorney Arthur I. "Buddy" Jacobs, the American Beach Property Owners' Association (ABPOA) under my administration was chartered and incorporated by the laws of the State of Florida. American Beach, Incorporated, also a 501(c)3 organization, was dissolved in the transformation. The purpose was to give the community and taxpaying property owners a direct voice regarding the community and their investments. In the beginning, the name change stirred much confusion among a few citizens, but turned out to be in the best interest of the community for grant writing and other sought after projects representing property owners. This proved to be an excellent move.

Into the 1990s, and continuing the declining years of American Beach, there continued an extensive effort by some citizens to take American Beach back to its heyday through the promotion of illegal commercial activities in the community, encouraging the hundreds of visitors from northeast Florida, Georgia, and elsewhere, who once came by tradition when there was no other beach for African-Americans.

Other citizens asked why? With the exception of a few Kuumba Festivals, an African-American arts and music event held at the mouth of Burney Park, there was no place for people to go and nothing to do except congregate in the vicinity of Lewis and Gregg Streets. There were no businesses open and the crowds seemed to ignore the ocean and Burney Park where there are picnic tables, outdoor shower facilities, and a county-maintained bathhouse with indoor shower and toilet facilities.

The still occasional large Sunday afternoon and holiday throngs of visitors were getting worse and taking things in the wrong direction.

These crowds were rowdy with plenty of teenagers in the mix, cussing, alcohol, drugs in the air, occasional fights, boom boxes sounding off, parking on private property, knocking down of private property fences, blocking driveways, open sex in plain view, open-air bars and negative publicity. This bad publicity not only affected American Beach, but Fernandina Beach, the county as a whole, and island tourism.[1]

This did not sit too well with families and others who took time out to enjoy an outing at the beach, and law-abiding citizens of the community.[2] The crowds did not realize American Beach was not what it once was, but it had now become a full blown respectable residential community with about thirty to forty families living year-round.

With help from county government and finding covenants and restrictions, complaints and persistence from citizens, law enforcement regarding open air bars, enforcement of noise and festival ordinances, tightening up on sexual abuse and drugs, the rowdy crowds eventually went away by the summer of 2002.

Those who came to enjoy the ocean continue to come. After all, the beachfront is a public beach open year round to everyone, but the neighborhood is not geared to partying crowds intent on destroying the community and contributing to the decline of American Beach.

1935   **AMERICAN BEACH**   1995

Founders' Day Observance

Saturday, January 21, 1995

4:00 p.m

Rev. J. Milton Waldron, D.D.   *Rev. E.J. Gregg, D.D.*

E.W. Latson   *Dr. A.L. Lewis*   *A.W. Price*
Chairman of Board of Directors

James Franklin Valentine   *Dr. Arthur Walls Smith*
Practicing Physician

Franklintown United Methodist Church

Lewis Street - American Beach, Florida

Sponsored by American Beach, Incorporated

The front cover of the American Beach 60th anniversary Founder's Day program in 1995.

Ground breaking, May 20, 2000, by governmental officials, American Beach officials, and a representative from Congresswoman Corrine Brown's office, for the Nassau County American Beach Community Center to be built at Mary Avenue and Julia Street.

Old time picnic, May 20, 2000, in celebration of the 65th anniversary, held at Burney Park, following the community center ground breaking and unveiling of the American Beach historic marker.

Association Projects

The Property Owners' Association initiated several community projects including the first *American Beach Founders' Day Observance* Saturday, January 21, 1995. This was the 60th anniversary.

The *Second and 65th Anniversary Founders' Day* was observed in the year 2000. On the same day, May 20, 2000, was the official ground breaking ceremony for the *Nassau County Community Center* to be erected at the corner of Julia Street and Mary Avenue, as well. County officials, the Chamber, AIP officials, community citizens, and others took part in this special event.

A lot of activity took place on this day. Marking the anniversary was the Dedication and Unveiling of a State Historic Marker, sited at the corner of Lewis and Waldron Streets, for the purpose of recognizing American Beach as a general interest site to the public in the State of Florida, and to those who are interested in the history of American Beach. Grant funding was in part from the Operating Trust Fund administered by the Florida Division of Historical Resources. Matching funds came from the Property Owners' Association. The marker was proudly erected for us by the Nassau County Public Works Department.

All these events culminated in an old time picnic in Burney Park on Burney Road in celebration of this eventful day.

Other Association Projects

What would American Beach look like today if there were no stately looking tropical palms lining our streets?

Three *State Forestry Grants* were initiated in 1993, 1994, 1995, and one local impact grant in 1998. These grants, written by our community grants writer, played a major role in helping to enhance the aesthetic appearance of the community giving it a more defined look, and generally improving the quality of life at American Beach. Over 200 cabbage palms, live oaks, and holly trees were planted by

James Robinson - 1995

State Forestry Grant and Beautification Enhancement Project. A shipment of cabbage palms that arrived in May 1995, ordered through Amelia Services, Inc., is being unloaded. The first shipment arrived in April 1994.

Community volunteers digging holes to plant palm trees. Maintenance and caretaker operating machinery. Project chairman, William Watson, far right.

James Robinson - 1995.

volunteers. We were fortunate to have a well organized 4-H group headed by dedicated community volunteers, who also did their share of landscaping. Overall, the community was working together quite harmoniously. There was enough to do for everyone to get involved and be a part of their community, and they did.

Apart from community volunteer services, contributions were made by Rayonier (mulch), White Oak Plantation (water tank), Amelia Island Plantation (equipment and manpower), Amelia Services, Inc. (equipment, manpower, planting, and watering), Fire and Rescue, Nassau County Public Works, and University of Florida Landscape Architect, Noel R. Lake.

Volunteers planting a palm tree.

James Robinson - 1995

Perhaps, the trees will continue to survive and be a part of our legacy in years to come, as the palms planted by slaves have continued to exist for hundreds of years at the nearby Kingsley Plantation, in Jacksonville, just south of Amelia Island.

Prior to the first forestry grant project, entrance signs were placed at the corner of Lewis Street and AIA, which helped to identify American Beach as the first stop on the Florida Black Heritage Trail of 141 sites throughout the state.

There were more accomplishments and improvements as time moved on. Sidewalks were installed by the county from AIA and Lewis Street to Gregg Street in 1993 to facilitate pedestrians' access to the ocean. Streets were paved and drainage improved for six additional streets through 1995. Lewis Street was widened from Mary Avenue to Ocean Boulevard. A pump station was installed by the county at the corner of Lewis Street and Ocean Boulevard to improve rain water drainage.

The Neighborhood Safety Patrol was funded through the Nassau County Sheriff's Department by the U. S. Department of Justice, set in motion July 30, 1996, and led by community citizen retired Deputy Sheriff Ben Sessions, sitting in the driver's seat. Sheriff Ray Geiger, sitting in the passenger's seat. This program is still operating in 2011.
James Robinson - November 1998

A fourth beach access boardwalk was installed by the county near Burney Park designed for wheelchair accessibility. An American Beach entrance sign was erected at State Road AIA and Burney courtesy of Osprey Village at Amelia Island Plantation.

The Neighborhood Crime Watch and Safety Patrol Program was established July 30, 1996, and led by a long time community citizen and retired county deputy sheriff. The program is still in operation today to help safeguard the community.

A $12,000 grant from the U.S. Department of Justice with matching funds from the Nassau County Sheriff's Office made the American Beach Safety Patrol Program a model for other neighborhoods to replicate.

American Beach entrance sign at Burney Road and SR AIA. The sign was installed March 10, 1999, compliments of Osprey Village at Amelia Island Plantation (AIP).

Photo by James Robinson - 1999

A new golf cart was donated to the association by our neighbors, the Ritz-Carlton Hotel, Amelia Island Plantation, and Summer Beach Resort, to provide mobility for the Watch Team to perform routine duties throughout the neighborhood.

With these projects and improvements, major Neighborhood Clean-Up Days were implemented with the help of Keep Nassau Beautiful, Sheriff's Department inmates, Nassau House, and the Nassau County Waste Department. Older homes were renovated, new homes were built, and abandoned, unsightly and unsafe homes and structures were removed. Speed limit, no parking, and zero tolerance drug signs were placed throughout the area, all contributing to an enhanced sense of community. Beachgoers then began to show greater respect for private properties and the community.

American Beach entrance sign placed at the corner of Lewis Street and State Highway A1A in 1993. Located in the background, near the entrance, is the Nassau County Fire and Rescue Station No. 20, and a new restaurant adjacent to the north side of the fire station. Lewis Street is the entrance to the first site on the Florida Black Heritage Trail.

James Robinson - February 1994

American Beach 4-H Club organized, December 26, 1992.
In photo, Frances Green, group leader and Annette Myers, president.

ABPOA and the community worked with Keep Nassau Beautiful (KNB) on clean-up days and volunteered to keep the beachfront cleaned. Sign posted at Burney Park.

James Robinson - 1997

James Robinson - January 14, 1997

Rayonier truck delivers mulch on the south end of Ocean Boulevard.

Bark mulch (35 tons/100 yards) donated by Rayonier to help with the tree planting project. Standing next to the truck are Rayonier representatives and American Beach officials.

James Robinson - January 14, 1997

Photos by the author - 1997

Cabbage palms along Lewis Street, paved sidewalk by the county completed, May 1993, and street widened in 1994. White building on the left once known as Duck's Ocean Vu-Inn, formally Lee's Ocean Vu-Inn.

Palms lining the road on the east end of Julia Street.

An American Beach volunteer, Maxcell Wilson, attends smaller trees on
Lewis Street and kept plants at the entrance of Lewis Street years before streetscape began.

Palms along the north end of Ocean Boulevard.

Photo by the Author - December 1998

Neighborhood Clean-Up in collaboration with the Nassau County Solid Waste Department. Homeowner Bobby Morgan-Jones, in the forefront.

Neighborhood Clean-Up.

Photo by the Author - December 1998

James Robinson - May 1996

Phillip Jefferson, 4-H President and Fernandina Beach High School graduating senior, receives award from American Beach President Annette Myers.

> "The function of government must be to fa-
> vor no small group at the expense of its duty
> to protect the rights of personal freedom and
> of private property of all its citizens."
> *(Franklin Delano Roosevelt)*

Chapter 4
National Register of Historic Places

The idea of establishing the American Beach enclave as a historic site is to protect this valuable and distinctive African-American coastal community from future incompatible development, and to ensure future generations the opportunity to see a pristine area that once served as a unique recreational retreat for African-Americans during the 1930s segregation era[1] to the present day.

The first step for placement on the National Register began with a Historical Survey by the ABPOA listing historically significant properties at American Beach, after receiving a matching grant awarded by the Florida Bureau of Historic Preservation. The survey identified properties constructed prior to 1947. There were thirty such buildings meeting that criterion.

The completed Survey Document was submitted to the Division of Historical Resources by the Association, December 14, 1998, to identify the total community for national recognition.

Between 1998 and January 2001, other supporting documents were submitted, homes were rephotographed and submitted, community workshops held, State Historical Resources representatives were invited to speak, and on-site visitations were made by the state recommending division.

I received a call from Tallahassee requesting a copy of the historical covenants and restrictions that went with the land for 50 years, a document that had expired January 1, 2000. This was the last document requested and forwarded by me, October 18, 2001. The covenants, established by the African-American Pension Bureau, August 19, 1949,

Annette Myers speaking to the congregation at the historic New Zion (Missionary) Baptist Church about American Beach, during Black History Month, February 1999.

state in nine paragraphs, inclusive, the boundaries of American Beach, how the land should be zoned and used, and general intentions for the community by the founders—the greater portion of the land to be used for dwelling houses in areas zoned residential. Certain lots and the A.L. Lewis Motel near the ocean were exempted from these restrictions and could be used for businesses—such as they were, but no large scale commercial development.[2]

According to our survey, the most effective legal tool available for the protection of historic sites is the local historic preservation ordinance. The exercise of governmental control over land use is essentially the prerogative of local government. In Florida, the home–rule law permits local government to exercise such authority. Unlike the City of Fernandina Beach, Nassau County did not have a historic preservation ordinance that would provide for protection of its historic resources.

Then came Monday night, April 12, 2004, when Nassau County Commissioners moved to approve an ordinance, as unanimously recommended

Building Our Community Historic Preservation Workshop with State Historic Bureau Preservation Chief Barbara Mattick and Historic Preservation Specialist Joel McEachin, held at the Fernandina Beach Golf Club.

James Robinson - September 20. 1997

by the Planning and Zoning Board, to protect the county's historic places and sites. Having virtually no discussion or hesitation among commissioners, the ordinance was passed. The county attorney cited how the ordinance noted economic benefits of historic preservation that also brings about historic interest and tourism. The ordinance outlines how historic buildings nominated and listed are protected from potentially damaging activities and surrounding development.[3]

The National Register of Historic Places is an official listing of properties throughout the country that reflect the prehistoric occupation and historic development of our nation, states, and total communities of buildings, sites, structures, and objects that are significant to our culture and historic heritage.[4]

American Beach attained National Register listing on January 28, 2002.

"What we call "progress" is the exchange of one
nuisance for another nuisance."
(Havelock Ellis)

"The biggest problem in the world could have
been solved when it was small."
(Witter Bynner)

"Those who speak of progress measure it by
quantity and not by quality."
(George Santayana)

Chapter 5

Water and Sewer Infrastructure

Since 1982, this has been one of the most discussed and on-going
issues among citizens of American Beach. Formal studies have taken
place, many workshops, and public hearings held.

Dating back to the 1930s, water lines were run throughout the
community providing water from the well located on property of the
A.L. Lewis Motel. It is now referred to as the "Historical Well."

For sewers, every household had septic tanks. As American Beach
began to develop, more homes were constructed and with the high
volume of water used during summer months by year-rounders and
vacationers, drawing water became a problem with the water less
than free flowing. Eventually, instead of the 120-some households
the central system once had, around 25 households now get their tap
water from the central well.[1] Other residents are on individual wells
and continue to use septic tanks.

American Beach is in the unincorporated area of Nassau County.
Unlike the City of Fernandina Beach, Nassau County has not been in
the business of serving its residents by either public water, or sewer
facilities. With the acquisition of Nassau Amelia Utilities in March of

2003,[2] the county now had the opportunity to provide water and sewer to American Beach and other areas. Before that happens, according to the county grants coordinator, the county had a "voluminous stack" of paperwork to apply for funding from the U.S. Department of Agriculture's rural development program for American Beach. An environmental assessment of the area was required plus public hearings.[3]

As of August 28, 2003, the area comprised 330 narrow lots with both paved and unpaved streets. The existing Amelia Island Utilities water and sewer system borders American Beach to the north, south, and west sides, and is said to have sufficient size and capacity to provide adequate service.[4]

The estimated price tag according to the engineering firm of Post, Buckley, Schue, and Jernigan was about $3.9 million or $11,921 per household. This cost did not include surveying, engineering, and administrative costs estimated at 15% - 20%, adding up to around $4 million.[5]

Property owners connecting to the sewer system would be required to abandon their septic tanks and re-pipe their sewer service to front property lines, normally accomplished by a plumbing contractor at an additional estimated cost of $2,000-$2,500 per connection.

1990 County CDBG Study and Grant Sought

A public hearing was advertised by the County, November 7, 1990, notifying citizens of an application to the Florida Department of Community Affairs (DCA), for a grant under the Neighborhood Small Cities Community Development Block Grant (CDBG) Program in the amount of $650,000. The purpose of this grant was redevelopment of the American Beach area, for the installation and hook-ups, for sanitary sewers, water lines, and fire hydrants, where at least 60% of the funds would benefit low to moderate income persons.[6] From information gathered, the community did not qualify based on income levels.

Another Grant Study

County Commission Meeting Minutes—Thursday, August 14, 1997—
Initial costs were to be in excess of $930,000 and the county could not
meet the projected cost of $650,000. Again, reason being, residents in
the area were not of the income level that would require the county
to meet this threshold and were higher in the income level.

Alternatives for the community have been to seek utility grants,
construction of a new cost-prohibitive central water system, connection for the existing nearest water lines along State Road A1A,
commercial financing, or upgrading the current central water system.

What property owners are saying about water and sewer: Residents, in polls or otherwise, have expressed mixed feelings about this
cost-prohibitive issue. In a "Building Our Communities" workshop in
November 1997, property owners heard the pros and cons of upgrading
their utilities from Florida Water Service and Gardnyr Michael, Capital,
Inc. The cost would be around $600,000 for a typical gravity sewer

Unpaved pristine side street at the north end of Lee Street.

Photo by the Author - November 1997

system and about $250,000 for water lines totaling more than $800,000.

Sewer lines would be more expensive for residents who live closer to the ocean. They would require a new system. Residents closer inland could connect to sewer lines already in place. A typical water bill in this area, we were told, is about $35 a month and sewer is about $50 or $60 a month. Additionally, each household would have to pay $3,500 in hook-up fees.[7]

Through the years and currently, residents are getting free water and sewer from their own wells and septic tanks. When tested by the association on December 9, 1996, through the Department of Health and Rehabilitative Services, well water proved to be good quality water. Those who have had problems with rust or lime have deep wells or water filtering systems.

Grant Funding Again Pursued [8]

Again, the county was informed in February 2004 of the community's ineligibility, for grant funding, because the area's average income is too high based on U.S. Census data. The census grouped American Beach with all Amelia Island neighborhoods south of Sadler Road.[9]

After 70-plus years, there has been no documented infiltration of pollutants in the drinking water. Some property owners are saying if it's not broken, why fix it, and who's having problems with their water or sewer? Others are saying the community has water, those who moved here knew the situation before they bought their properties, public water is not going to be any better than the water we are currently getting, most impurities are found from 0 to 25 or 30 feet, all wells for serving households are deeper than 25 or 30 feet, the plantation golf courses will poison our water, or with more development our septic tanks must be at least 75 feet from an existing well under current codes. See Chapter 6 CRA.

> "The power of perpetuating our property in
> our families is one of the most valuable and
> interesting circumstances belonging to it, and
> that which tends the most to the perpetuation
> of society itself."
>
> *(Edmond Burke, 1729-1797)*

Chapter 6

The Threat of a Community Redevelopment Agency (CRA)

The CRA, a heated topic, first came to the community's attention through a news article in the Real Estate section of the *New York Times*, January 24, 1999.* This media coverage was shocking to the association and the community. The article mentioned a Jacksonville African-American banker and recent property owner on the beach no one seemed to know, someone unknown to me as association president, someone we were introduced to through the news article, and someone who claimed that he wanted to do much to preserve American Beach. Yet he was someone who wanted to persuade other property owners to create an American Beach CRA.

Eventually, we met the banker who found members of the Property Owners' Association wary of his persuasion to endorse his draft proposals for neighborhood revitalization. The banker's plan offered several options to finance capital improvements such as water and sewer utilities through tax increment financing, so property tax increases would be directed back to the neighborhood to fund improvements. It was a strange feeling. From time to time, people came along with their own ideas about our community. For this reason and early on, we did not trust this stranger before agreeing to work with him. Ultimately, his proposals would have to go before the local county governing body for approval.

* CRAs across the country are controversial as local officials have the authority to issue bonds without a vote of the people, buy private property from unwilling owners through eminent domain, and place other restrictions and difficult choices upon older communities and older Americans.

The community concerns were many, including the practicality and feasibility of a CRA for a neighborhood made up of residential and single family homes such as American Beach, whether the community alone could generate the funds needed, or a district tie-in would be required to adjacent communities, for the plan to be effective. The community needed to know that they must be involved and understand who pays for infrastructure improvements, under what terms and predictable foreseeable risks involved to their investments, the increases in property values and taxes generated due to redevelopment, and the benefits of a CRA as opposed to a Community Development District (CDD). Generally, the community felt that the unincorporated portion of the island has been relatively undeveloped and there is no need for "redevelopment." Residents and property owners were not willing to give in to the potential risks of having a CRA as opposed to the perceived benefits a CRA would bring.

Following my ten-year tenure in office, the CRA was strongly pursued by the incoming administration with a minority representation of less than 20% of some two hundred and thirty property owners. Citizens were saying that this did not fairly represent a majority of property owners, which resulted in numerous workshops, studies, and public hearings.

I understood CRA's findings of necessity dealt with deteriorated sites and structures, underused lots, land use conflicts, lack of infrastructure—mainly public water and sewer—lack of affordable housing, and "A Determination of Blight" as defined in Chapter 163, Part III of the Florida Statutes to be a part of the process.

Neither I nor others could see or understand declaring American Beach blighted for the convenience of developers, the threat of losing

* In recent times, as late as June 2005, a 5-4 Supreme Court decision spurred many issues and controversies where cities have the power to bulldoze people's homes to make way for shopping malls or other developments. The ruling gives local governments a wide range of power to seize private properties to generate tax dollars for economic development and to decide what is best for a community. The decision, according to retired Justice Sandra Day O'Connor, who dissented the ruling, said the decision "bowed to the rich and powerful at the expense of middle-class Americans." [1]

our investments, and eventually being kicked out, or forced out by eminent domain.* So why should we be foolish enough to force our descendants and ourselves out by opening the floodgate to developers and large-scale development?

The CRA resolution presented by the association to Nassau County Commissioners was approved in December 2001.

This sparked an overwhelming two-year battle between the association and the community and nearly tore the community apart.

About a month later in January 2002, American Beach was added to the National Register of Historic Places.

There was a strong general consensus by the community and voices heard that the community was not blighted, but needed a good cleaning up, continued streetscape, emphasis needed by playing up historical preservation aspects, improved entrance, street signage, banners, much needed cosmetic improvements from private property owners, and freedom of developing their vacant lots in a timely manner as they saw fit without being forced to develop or forced out. Opposers saw the CRA as a threat and another way to expediently lose pieces of American Beach.

The community had concerns that no other unincorporated community in the county had been declared blighted for CRA development, as most unincorporated areas are on private wells and septic tanks, anyway, with the exception of private developments and gated communities.

Lack of affordable housing did not fit on this resort end of the island when lots were selling in excess of $100,000 and $500,000, and where some individuals own two or more homes.

To take care of deteriorated buildings, the county has in place zoning codes and regulations already in progress to address the issue for unsafe buildings and health hazards.

Land Use Conflicts Call for Special District Zoning Overlay

An original overlay developed for American Beach by professional experts[2] that historically characterized the coastal community, such as maintaining original density, original use, building heights, and lot coverage, was presented to the county in 1998. This was designed to be a road map to guide future development of the area. Since there were so many concerns by a few property owners after repeated workshops, meetings, and hearings, the association under my administration dropped the issue.

In December 2002, the zoning overlay, with changes, was brought back by the succeeding administration to Nassau County Commissioners, after more meetings and hearings. The overlay to maintain the area's historical integrity by governing the size and appearance of future construction and aid in maintaining an unobstructed ocean view [3] also opened up to multi-family dwellings that may now be non-conforming, townhouses and duplexes in residential areas, and other new changes some property owners felt would affect them.

The controversial overlay was again addressed by members of the community. Changes made without the community's consent were the pronounced issue. However, the Special District Zoning Overlay, 2002-63, was ultimately passed by commissioners and established by the county, December 16, 2002.[4] This was met with favoritism for those who wanted the ordinance passed and for those who wanted to see American Beach move into the 21st century.[5]

My concern for American Beach, unlike Summer Beach and Amelia Island Plantation, is to become its own quaint village using a 1995 Conceptual Planning Study[6] as a guide preserving much of the original character as endorsed by the founders.

Once the character of the community changes by CRA development, the community is no longer historical. I expressed before the Nassau County Commissioners Board in 2004 and at other times that "either we are for historic preservation or CRA development, and I don't believe the two go hand in hand for American Beach. Once development comes in, we lose control of the community. Once we lose control, the community is gone."

CRA opponents expressed their feelings in other ways by staking "Say No To CRA" signs throughout the community.

Other expressions I heard at county meetings, community meetings, and through personal conversations...

"Why don't we put a nail in the coffin and forget it. Forget about eminent domain and forget about the CRA."[7]

"There is no mandate that restricts the proper use of septic tanks."

"Any plan that accelerates growth and increase in taxes is not in the best interest of representing the constituents at American Beach."

"One man's blight is another man's beauty. A historic ordinance would protect the historic interests of American Beach."[8]

A lawsuit contesting the blighted designation significantly impacted the CRA proposal.

Finally, Monday night on February 9, 2004, Nassau County Commissioners, in their vision and through persistence and vigilance of community citizens and owners, voted to repeal the CRA resolution. Lead association officials who pushed for the proposal are now saying, "The proposal is divisive and might not justify what is happening in the community, and due to the county's stepped-up efforts for exploring avenues for water and sewer." Other property owners felt the CRA would endanger the community by encouraging large-scale and fast-paced growth and development.[9] The community stood steadfast to see the CRA rescinded.

From my perspective, whatever plan is put in place, we must assure that everyone is assessed equally and fairly, not only homeowners, but every property owner.

"The only dependable foundation of personal
liberty is the personal economic security of
private property."

(Walter Lippmann)

Chapter 7

Historic Survey of American Beach for National Register

Buildings documented in American Beach under our 1998 historic survey study for the National Registry, were constructed over a thirty-year period between 1935 and 1965. With a few exceptions, the buildings tended to be constructed in simpler forms and lacked the distinctive style definition, or the architectural detailing characteristics of buildings constructed during the first quarter of the 20th century.[1]

James Robinson - November 1997

*Row of American Beach Community homes along the Atlantic
Oceanfront. The early home of A.L. Lewis sits to the left.
The home was restored serveral years ago under new ownership.*

New Zion Baptist Church. Built in 1907 under the supervision of William "Billy" Rivers. The church auditorium has the largest seating capacity of any church in Fernandina Beach. New Zion has been used for Peck High School graduations and other community activities. It is still used for community activities to this day. A State Historical Marker was dedicated and unveiled at the site, November 18, 2001.

Photo by the Author - April 2003

Because of the inclusion of buildings constructed after the fifty-year criteria established by the National Park Service, many buildings exemplified the use of materials such as concrete block, metal-frame windows, and exterior siding, or synthetic materials not typically associated with the historic period ending in the immediate post-war period. Further, the majority of buildings documented as being constructed in the historic period tended to have some degree of alteration, in some cases, to the extent they lost virtually all of their original character. In response to the corrosive beach environment and to reduce maintenance expenses, some alterations included the use of artificial sidings such as asbestos, tiles, vinyl, aluminum or stucco finish, as well as the replacement of original wooden double-hung, or casement windows with aluminum or vinyl clad windows, or jalousie windows.[2]

Of the 86 buildings documented in American Beach proper, fourteen were associated with the Depression/New Deal Era (1929-1941), twenty-three with World War II and aftermath (1941-1950), and the greater majority, forty-nine, were associated with the Modern era (1950-present). By decades, these totals break down as ten in the 1930s, twenty-two in the 1940s, thirty-two in the 1950s, and twenty-two between 1960 and 1964. Because of its style and materials, the house at 5401 James Street was probably constructed before the 1930s, and later relocated to American Beach.[3]

Completed in August of 1935 for A.L. Lewis, the house at 5466 Gregg Street, later sold to his son, was documented to be the first house constructed in American Beach by local well-known contractor William S. Rivers.* The second home immediately next door at 5472 Gregg Street was constructed for A.L. Lewis in 1938. Another early vacation

---

* Rivers was responsible for the construction of a pavilion and six cabins (no longer standing) constructed for the Pension Bureau of the Afro-American Life Insurance Company at American Beach [5] on the northeast end of Julia Street.

William Rivers, known as "Billy" Rivers, and also a known boat builder, is credited with the construction of New Zion Baptist Church located in the historic district of downtown Fernandina Beach of which I am a lifetime member and church historian. The original New Zion Church was destroyed by fire in 1907 and rebuilt the same year under Mr. Rivers' supervision. The church remains unchanged to this day.

home built in American Beach was for one of the Afro-American Insurance Company founders, Louis D. Ervin, at 5448 Gregg Street.[4]

Of the American Beach historic survey study in 1998, in addition to Ervin's Rest, two other buildings over fifty years old without significant structural changes and potentially eligible for private listing on the National Register of Historic Places were Martha's Hideaway and Duck's Ocean Vu-Inn. Also, the Franklin Town Cemetery was a potential site.[6]

James Robinson - 1995

Ervin's Rest. The first home on the National Register listed April 23, 1998.[7] The photo was taken sometime prior, before home was registered. Shown is the east end of Julia Street at Gregg Street, view of the Atlantic Ocean, Julia Street boardwalk beach access, and the planted palms on Julia Street.

"Property is the fruit of labor; property is
desirable; it is a positive good."
(Abraham Lincoln, 1809-1865)

Chapter 8

Martha's Hideaway

During the early phase of development on American Beach, construction of a few private homes was begun.

One of the first homes hidden deep in the woods, at the end of Ervin Street, was a home built for local well-known business owner and community activist Martha Hippard. Also known to be the richest black woman in Fernandina, she operated a restaurant and lounge called Plum Garden on North Third Street, left of Centre Street, in the heart of downtown Fernandina. Lemuel Hippard, Miss Martha's first husband, and she also owned and operated a bakery and grocery store in the building.[1] My colleagues and I would go to North Third Street in the evenings to the open roof top lounge. My parents were strict, but now I was grown and could go just about anywhere I wanted to go.

I remember my late husband taking me to the restaurant when we were courting in the 1950s. As a teenager, I would go to North Third Street on special occasions to get my hair done in the adjacent beauty parlor building.

Miss Martha's American Beach home was constructed after the passing of her first husband, then the 1936[2] loss of her second husband, Griffin Simmons, and her daughter, Sarah Hippard, in a tragic automobile accident. Detached from the main grandiose house was a separate party house that some say was a gambling house.

The party house, according to others, was used to host dances, club parties, other civic and social activities, and religious activities. I questioned the religious activities after finding certain historical archives (bottles) buried in the woods behind the party house.

What's unusual about the house is that it was constructed of hand-hewn concrete blocks manufactured in the yard from truckloads of coquina shells hauled from the beach and hand molded bricks, built on nearly one acre of continuous land, more than any other single family home owner or property owner in the area had acquired.

The best craftsmen in Fernandina were hired to build the house. A German craftsman by the name of Frank Xavier Mayer of Sonthofer, Germany, who migrated along with his wife to Fernandina in 1936 (1903-1993), is credited with the carpentry work on the house and did repairs on the home during his lifetime. The two-story masonry house was constructed by a well-known African-American contractor, Frank Johnson, whose family had first settled in the New Berlin area of Duval County before moving to Fernandina Beach in the 1870s (died 1962). Johnson, along with his young son Frank Johnson, Jr., constructed the blocks by hand on site by mixing a formula of one part cement with two parts coquina making two blocks at a time and pouring the mixture into two 16" x 8" x 8" molds. The blocks were then removed from the molds and sun dried in the yard.[3] Birdie Delaney of the Delaney family, according to my mother, did the brick work on the house and chimney.

Miss Martha's father, Brooks Thompson,* who was known for

Martha's Hideaway, built 1938, as it looks today. The party house to the left was converted into a two-car garage for new adaptive use.   Photo by the Author

wood carved furniture, left his daughter with beautiful pieces of hand carved furniture. Pieces of his furniture are owned by the Myers family and other pieces exist in the family of the retired Nassau County Tax Collector Gwendolyn Miller, given to Mrs. Miller during her childhood by Miss Martha.[4]

The second owner of the Hippard beach house, Lottie Orleana Harris, a single woman of St. Marys, Georgia and a prominent educator throughout the State of Georgia, came in possession of the house in 1953, reportedly in a gambling debt encumbered by the original owner Martha Hippard.[5]

Elmo Myers, my husband of 30 years and a well-known commercial seaman from St. Marys, Georgia, and I, a school teacher of Fernandina, honeymooned at the Hideaway in 1956. The house was sometimes used for this purpose, and to accommodate other vacationing family and friends of "Miss Lottie," as she was often called.

While on our honeymoon the house was offered to us, as Miss

*Nassau County National Association for the Advancement of Colored People (NAACP) got its start in the year 1925 by Brooks Thompson, an ex-slave, and his daughter Martha Hippard. During that period, Mr. Thompson was the champion of Black people and their causes in Nassau County. In 1925, Mr. Thompson and Martha formed an organization called "The Cotton Climate Claims," which later became the Nassau County Branch of NAACP.[6]

*Zora Neale Hurston (1891-1960),[7] folklorist, anthropologist and author, visited the area and married Works Progress Administration (later known as Works Projects Administration/WPA) Education Department employee Albert Price, III in Fernandina at the Nassau County Courthouse, June 27, 1939.[8] Albert III was grandson of Alfred W. Price, Sr., one of the founders of the Afro-American Life Insurance Company.[9] Hurston is also reported to have stayed in the home of Brooks Thompson, Miss Martha's father, as she collected forklore and folktales in the Franklin Town area.[10]

**As a property owner, I knew the owner of Evans' Rendezvous, Willie B. Evans, as the president of the American Beach Homeowner Association. In a letter I received May 22, 1967, he states in part: "Dear Property Owner: We know you are interested in the development of our American Beach because of your purchase of property here. We want to develop our beach as one of the finest communities in our area and this will only be possible through the best efforts of all concerned. A meeting of all property owners will be held in the Lounge of the A.L. Lewis Motel on Tuesday, May 30th at 8:00 p.m. Signed— Yours truly, W.B. Evans, President.[11]

Miss Martha, first owner (right), and friend Hanna Mitchell vacationing in Havana, Cuba in the late 1940s. The picture was presented to me several years ago by Marsha Phelts.

Lottie also knew Elmo Myers' kinfolks very well, a prominent family of St. Marys. She said she would only sell to us, or the owner of Evans' Rendezvous at that time.** A few years later Miss Lottie sent word to me again by my in-laws.

The Myers--third owners--began our purchase of the house and furniture about five years later between 1959-1961 and completed the deal in January 1961, after I made a special Christmas visit to Georgetown, British Guiana, in South America, December 1960, to get down to the nuts and bolts of the investment with Elmo Myers,

Lottie O. Harris, the second owner of the house on Ervin Street, built by Martha Hippard. Photo - Courtesy Dr. Ann Harris Stoddard.

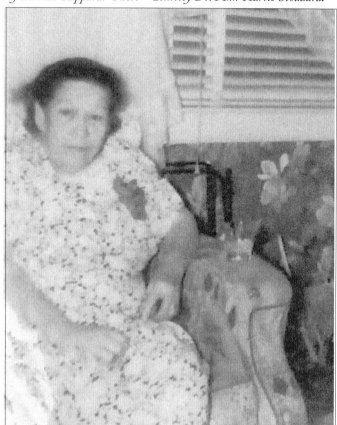

who was working off the waters of Guiana.

While Elmo was away in South America, and as I traveled back and forth between Fernandina and Georgetown, I was afraid to live in the house alone. Rumors had it that Miss Lottie kept coffins in the attic and under the stairs. There were coffins in her house in St. Marys. Sure enough, I saw them with my own eyes in her attic. They were for herself and family members. I attended the funeral of her sister who died later, after her. She was buried in one of the coffins. Since Miss Lottie was a seller of coffins,[8] the story was extended to include this house. To this day, I have yet to find them here.

What a scare that was![9] Some years after that, when I actually

Elmo and Annette Myers, the third owners of the home built on Ervin Street by Martha Hippard. Photo taken at our home in Guiana, 1965.

began to live in the house, and after living in Guiana for a few years, a little girl came to live with me by the name of Aerial. I was glad her Mama let her come, because I was still somewhat afraid to stay in the house alone.

Hippard's Hideaway, as it is referred to today, is a palatial Colonial Revival style two-story single-family residential home. Detached from the main grandiose house is a separate party house, which was converted by the Myers family into a two-car garage.

On December 14, 1998, an application to place Hippard's Hideaway on the National Register was submitted. Finally on October 12, 2001, nearly three years later, with the help of historic site specialist Joel McEachin of Jacksonville, Florida, and State Historic Site Specialist Robert Jones of Tallahassee, Florida, Martha Hippard's Hideaway was officially listed on the National Register of Historic Places.

Still secluded today, the house retains much of its original splendor and character with some adaptable living cosmetic changes, window shutters, new furniture and plumbing fixtures, and sits on exactly one acre of land. One big change to the house today is the burglar bars covering all windows, a sign of the times.

A celebration was held January 23, 2002, at the historic New Zion Missionary Baptist Church in recognition of the Hideaway's National Register listing. Descendants of Frank Johnson, relatives of Birdie Delaney, relatives of Lottie O. Harris, wife and families of Frank Mayer, the Myers families, my American Beach neighbors, New Zion Church affiliates, and many other relatives and friends were included and attended this momentous celebration. A proclamation was presented from the Office of Congresswoman Corrine Brown along with the National Register of Historic Sites Certificate. A resolution from the Nassau County Board of County Commissioners was presented by the commissioner, at that time, David Howard, who also represented the American Beach District.

Elmo Myers. Photo taken in Georgetown, Guiana, in 1961.

At our house in Guiana is Elmo with Antonio Carey, my nephew. He lived with us in Guiana from 1964 (five months old) to 1966, when we all finally returned to the United States.

A house we lived in, in Georgetown. After my first visit in the summer of 1960, I visited again, December 1960, July 1962, and lived there from June 1964 up to Guiana's independence, June 1966. Elmo Myers leaning over the veranda.

Elmo Myers, commercial sea captain, on the shrimp vessel he navigated from the United States, Tampa, Florida, to Guiana. Photo taken in 1965.

Georgetown, British Guiana, downtown district, 1966. British Guiana, also known as the Land of Six Peoples, was a British colony until its independence in May 1966. After independence, the name Georgetown, Guyana, was adopted.

Collection of the Author - Photo by Vivian McDonald / The Daily Chronicle (Guyana)

Independence Celebration in Guiana. Queen Elizabeth and the Duke of Edinburgh in the royal limo. Elmo, Antonio, and I are somewhere in the crowd.

Collection of the Author - Photo by Vivian McDonald / The Daily Chronicle (Guyana)

Illuminated Town Hall. For the Independence Celebration in Guiana in 1966, the downtown buildings and stores were lighted.

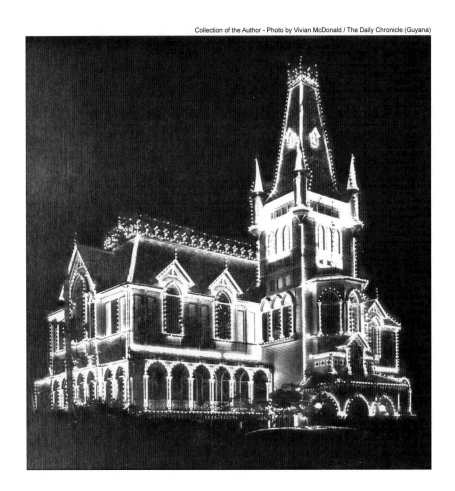

James Robinson 1997

Book signing at the Myers home, Martha's Hideaway, for Marsha Phelts, July 5, 1997. We are standing behind the desk hand crafted by Miss Martha's father, Brooks Thompson.

Gerald Roberts - August 2005

A Myers family heirloom, now in the home of Thelma Myers of St. Marys, Georgia. The table is another piece of furniture hand carved by Brooks Thompson.

*Donald Myers and his Savannah College
girlfriend Dedria Roberts of Augusta,
Georgia. Dedria visited the Hideaway during
their courtship before they married, July 1,
2000, in Augusta, Georgia. Photo - Courtesy
Donald and Dedria Myers.*

My son, Donald, who grew up at the beach and his cousins, Tony, Wendell, and Chris Carey. They are celebrating Donald's 8th birthday at Martha's Hideaway. Photo taken December 12, 1978.

Aerial Wilson (far right) lived in the Myers' home on the beach. Photo taken in December 1967. Aeriel now goes by Alria Wilson Mundy (married name).

"In every society where property exists there will ever be a struggle between rich and poor. Mixed in one assembly, equal laws can never be expected; they will either be made by the members to plunder the few who are rich, or by the influential to flee the many who are poor."

(John Adams)

Chapter 9

American Beach – Now Boxed In[1]

Over time, American Beach consisted of a total of 216 acres and approximately one-half mile, or two thousand feet of oceanfront. As other parts of Nassau County, S.R. AIA, Amelia Island, and other historical communities are being discovered and developed, so is the African-American coastal community of American Beach.

A blue-and-black color undated brochure circulated in the 1970s by the Amelia Island Plantation assured investors the adjacent African-American Beach community did not seem destined to keep its special identity much longer, and in five years would be unrecognizable as it would change from"black beach" to "beach" and be absorbed and blended into surrounding development. "Further, the need it once served would now be gone."[2]

In 1970, the Amelia Island Company began to purchase property on the south end of Amelia Island, including the 1872 century-old properties and self-sufficient community of slave descendants of Franklin Town, for the development of an extensive, gated resort community. The company also purchased property along Lewis Street near State Road AIA for the construction of a warehouse and maintenance facility for their new resort called Amelia Island Plantation.[3]

In 1972,[4] the Franklin Town families, who are currently watching history repeat itself, and their United Methodist Church were relocated one mile north to American Beach. They live in the first block of homes along Lewis Street and near the Amelia Island Plantation's unwanted warehouse and maintenance facility. Some families relocated near American Beach in a self-established community called Stewartville, and other families relocated to other areas. The historic Franklin Town Cemetery located on the west side of State Road AlA just south of American Beach remains in its original location. However, due to surrounding upscale development, the cemetery has been reduced from two acres to about one-half acre.[5]

According to an undated Annotated Chronology for the Plantation Park Project by Amelia Island Plantation, the Amelia Island Company and fourth owners acquired the nearly one-hundred-acre parcel along Burney Road in 1994-95. This was American Beach property sold by the A.L. Lewis family in the early 1980s. This original but undeveloped part of American Beach reduced the community to some 125 acres. It was cleared for the construction of a nine-hole golf course and sixty homes, which became an assisted living facility development called Osprey Village.

In addition to Amelia Island Plantation on the south, the remaining 125 acres of American Beach have since been surrounded by Summer Beach and Ritz-Carlton resorts on the north, and Plantation Point and Florence Point developments on the west across State Road AlA. The remaining 125 acres of American Beach have not attracted major resort development, evident to the north, south, and west, because most properties are small lots, about 50 feet by 100 feet (some more or less), controlled by a multitude of about 200 different owners from far and near, some owning multiple lots. However, these new resort developments have resulted in an increase in property values in the general area making it difficult to attract and keep middle class ownership.[6]

More than a third of beachfront lots, and some properties in the community, have been purchased by whites. Sales to whites and affluent blacks, who want to rival anything whites have but owned by blacks, have set higher property values which have continued to go up since the 1990s.[7] As property values keep climbing, my generation

---

* In the 1960s, beachfront lots were going for $4,000 to $6,000.

James Robinson - November 1997

(Top) The south end of American Beach from the very top of the 60-foot dune overlooking the community, Atlantic Ocean, and the former A.L Lewis Motel, now called American Beach Villas. Burney Park is the blue building to the right, and Amelia Island Plantation, far right, is seen to the extreme south. The tall red remodeled building was formerly called Dad and Chicks.

Full view of the former A.L. Lewis Motel from the top of the big sand dune.

James Robinson - November 1997

is surviving, yet there are some of us who are struggling to hold on. I am concerned about the next younger generation--our sons and daughters, and other kinship.

In 2005, beachfront lots were selling for in excess of $500,000 and they are continuing to increase as realtors report activities in the area and solicit other properties for sale.* Some properties belonging to heirs or multiple owners have fallen into disrepair and are being scooped up by both affluent blacks and whites looking to invest.

Other properties have been lost through county auctions and acquired by others due to non-payment of property taxes.

As the 60-foot tall NaNa, the tallest natural and untouched dune system on Amelia Island--located on American Beach consisting of 8.5 acres along with other adjacent property along Burney Road--was purchased by Amelia Island Plantation in 1994-95, for development of Osprey Village,[8] resort planners vowed to keep the dune in its natural vegetative state.[9] Some American Beach residents did not trust their promise.

Full view of the 60-foot dune, called NaNa, facing east on Ocean Boulevard. The dune is the tallest dune system on Amelia Island/Fernandina Beach. Through the years, the dune has suffered from some erosion.

James Robinson - January 1997

Photo by the Author - July 14, 2005

Franklintown United Methodist Church. The 1949 church was moved to the rear, used as a fellowship hall, and a new church built. Next door, far right and on American Beach, is a privately owned storage facility where a 150-foot telecommunications tower is located that the community opposed in 1998-99.

Photo by the Author - 1999

The cell tower that was sited on American Beach, Lewis Street.

AIP warehouse and maintenance facility on Lewis Street.   Photo by the Author - July 14, 2005

Convenience store and gas station at the left entrance of American Beach, Lewis Street. The Park Place of Amelia Island complex (shops and restaurants) is shown north of the convenience store.

Photo by the Author - 2005

Photo by the Author - July 14, 2005

The Ritz-Carlton parking lot at the west end of Julia Street, the entrance to American Beach.

A new development at the west end of Julia Street.

Photo by the Author - July 19, 2005

In February 2003, the plantation offered to donate the dune to the National Park Service in honor of the American Beach heritage and MaVynee Betsch, community activist, sand dune advocate, and great-granddaughter of Abraham Lincoln (A.L.) Lewis. Though the dune is some four miles north and not adjacent to the Timucuan Preserve, Florida H.R. 3768 was introduced by Congressman Ander Crenshaw and ultimately signed into law by President George W. Bush, September 2004. This allowed the National Park Service to accept the land by modifying boundaries of the Timucuan Ecological and Historic Preserve.[10]

The Timucuan Preserve was established by Congress in 1988 to protect one of the last unspoiled coastal wetlands on the Atlantic coast and to preserve historic and prehistoric sites on the Atlantic coast.[11]

Although no longer owned by American Beach, this piece of land that many of us have played on and explored as children will be preserved. *

As time goes on, the community still continues to shrink in size and, little by little, it continues to shift from ownership by African-Americans. In 2005, another prime piece of "heyday" beachfront property has been sold, but considered to be a worthwhile project. The acquisition is the historic Rendezvous building and property. The Florida Communities Trust state preservation program will pay $2.4 million for the purchase of the property. The 200-foot shoreline property will be held by the Trust until the county receives grant funding for ownership of the land. The state grant program was to reimburse Nassau County up to $3.2 million for the American Beach Park project in the 2005 grant cycle to conserve this historic landmark.[13] I understand the building will become a community center and cultural museum if it is salvageable, or torn down for a picnic pavilion if it cannot be saved. Also in the making was the proposed county services building at the corner of Mary Avenue and Julia Street, which was to include space for an American Beach museum. County officials, the community grant writer, association officials, and I broke ground for the county building, May 20, 2000, where construction was to begin

*"This is an ideal situation, putting a willing property donor and a willing caretaker together to preserve our history." Congressman Crenshaw.[12]

Ocean view and commercial area where crowds congregated. The red one-story brick building was known as Evans' Rendezvous.

James Robinson - 1997

(Bottom) View of the community from the big sand dune at Lewis Street and Ocean Boulevard. The Summer Beach Development is seen to the far north adjacent to American Beach. The white building next to the "Beach Lady's" trailer was El-Patio—no longer standing. (The blue house is Ervin's Rest). Other businesses opening in later years were William's Quick Snack—the red and white building at the corner of Lewis Street and Ocean Boulevard, and Little Zeng and Net's Place—the yellow buildings on Ocean Boulevard.

James Robinson - November 1997

in 2005, according to the County Building Maintenance Director.[13] Construction finally began in 2009 and was completed in 2010.

The Amelia Island Plantation sometime ago expressed their interest in the property at Mary Avenue and Julia Street. It is believed by some property owners that the plantation has always wanted this land.

Since the acquisition of the big sand dune NaNa by the National Park Service, one more large piece of endangered and undeveloped tract of land remains at American Beach. This parcel of land separated from NaNa by Ocean Boulevard called "Little NaNa," a three-acre sand dune at Burney Road and Ocean Boulevard across from Burney Park, has been for sale to anyone with the money to buy and is open to development. If the land is developed, this piece of the sand dune system will be plowed down for construction, and another piece of American Beach might be lost.

American Beach is a heritage worth preserving, but overshadowed by conflicts often within itself between some residents and owners who want to preserve the community as a quiet residential community, and

The Park Place office and retail complex is located next door to the Franklintown Church on Lewis Street.

Photo by the Author - August 1999

others who want to market the community, or work with developers to enhance and promote growth.[15] In September of 1994, the Property Owners' Association requested a feasibility study to identify activities for general community enhancement and to give the community a course of direction. Since the June 1995 Conceptual Planning Study and Feasibility Study prepared by Landers-Atkins Planners, Incorporated, through funding from Amelia Island Plantation, was completed and presented to the community several years ago, some projects have been implemented such as cabbage palms, live oaks, and holly trees, entrance signs at Lewis Street and Burney Road, roadway directional signs, private property improvements, street paving, private trash collection services, street banners, and other improvements as addressed in chapter three.

Overall, the few strands of American Beach—from 216 acres now down to about 100-plus acres—are looking better and more defined with improvement of private properties, and gradual construction of modest single-family homes within the last ten to fifteen years. Owners of single-family residential homes have basically preserved the community within the past 70-some years and as property owners struggle to keep their properties within family boundaries.

Photo by the Author - July 14, 2005

A closer view of AIP is seen to the south of American Beach.

A beautiful new home on Ocean Boulevard and Lewis Street.
New York owners - Sherald and Lois Wilson.

Photo by the Author - July 14, 2005

Photo by the Author - July 6, 2005

*Proposed site for the County Building—American Beach Community
Center—at Mary Avenue and Julia Street. Photo shows new housing development (villas)
at the west entrance of Julia Street.*

Curtis Davis - July 6, 2005

*A closer view of
the community
center proposed
site sign.*

A modest home built in recent times. Home of the Bridgewaters of Jacksonville, Florida.

Beachy looking home of Gwen Leapheart of Jacksonville, Florida, and the Burwells of New York.

Photo by the Author - 2006

A Julia Street home restored in 1994 by acquired owner Eve Jones, a retired physician's assistant from Philadelphia, who now lives on American Beach.

New structures on the south end of American Beach.

Photo by the Author - July 14, 2005

"The land shall not be sold forever: for the
land is mine; for ye are strangers and sojourn-
ers with me."

(Leviticus XXV. 23)

Chapter 10

Sunshine State

An independent fictionalized movie "Sunshine State," released in 2002
by writer-director John Sayles and producer Maggie Renzi, was filmed
in areas of Nassau County and at American Beach. The movie, star-
ing Angela Bassett, Timothy Hutton, and Edie Falco of HBO's *The
Sopranos,* depicts a true account of what our Franklin Town residents
relocated to American Beach have already experienced, resulting from
development at Amelia Island Plantation.

Director John Sayles chose to film his movie in Fernandina Beach
and American Beach, after he discovered American Beach and Amelia
Island and believed they fit perfectly with the movie's story in an area
facing development.[1]

Lincoln Beach, in the movie, parallels our own experiences and
struggles at American Beach, of valuable coastal property eyed daily
by greedy-eyed, chop-licking developers, and the second time around
for Franklin Town descendants.

In the past and in recent times, many articles have appeared in
local and other news media, far and wide, about American Beach as
they relate to this chapter:

"A heritage worth preserving." *St. Petersburg Times*, September 17, 1991.

Bigbee, Ivy. "The Rise, Fall and Future of American Beach."
    Folio Weekly, April 7, 1992.

Clary, Mike. "Preservationists cherish beach's black heritage." *Los
    Angeles Times,* September 24, 1998.

Davey, Monica. "Resorts close in on 'our little mecca.'" *St. Petersburg
    Times,* September 18, 1995.

Genz, Michelle. "Pride and Prejudice - Reports of Demise Premature." *Miami Herald-Tropic Magazine,* September 30, 1990.

Laird, Susan. "American Beach Reaches for its Glory Days." *Emerge,* September 1996.

Navarro, Mireya. "A Black Beach Town Fights to Preserve Its History." *The New York Times,* April 6, 1998.

Pittman, David. "American Beach soon to get office/retail park as neighbor." *Fernandina Beach News-Leader,* July 22, 1998.

"Residents have chance to communicate." Editorial. *Fernandina Beach News-Leader,* February 12, 1997.

Sharp, Deborah. "Waves of change beat upon beach community." *USA Today,* July 21, 1998.

Skokna, Christopher. "American Beach residents don't agree on its future." *Fernandina Beach News-Leader,* c.1996-97.

Tanner, Jane. "Is Change Coming?" *Florida Trend Magazine,* June 1999.

Turner, Kevin. "No to CRA on American Beach." *Fernandina Beach News-Leader,* February 11, 2004.

Wakefield, Vivian. "Families vow to preserve community." *The Florida Times-Union,* January 18, 1995.

Wakefield, Vivian, and Monica Richardson. "Heyday at American Beach gone, not forgotten." *Florida Times-Union,* February 11, 1996.

Williams, Mike. "Blacks hit the beach in battle to save heritage/ Owners in black resort vow never to sell." *The Atlanta Journal and Constitution,* February 10, 1991.

As days go by and on any given day, ritzy looking folks driving ritzy looking automobiles who appear to be looking for land to buy, or for other reason(s), are constantly riding around scrutinizing and sizing up the neighborhood and, according to others, circling this gold mine like vultures. Some have come for community tours and end up buying property as well.

As development continues to eat from the outside inward, many

American Beach shareholders are trying to hold on to their investments and their heritage. Other property owners are willing to sell if the price is right.

Those who want to preserve what is left of American Beach have worked together by pooling their time and resources to preserve the unique historical heritage and character of the only African-American coastal community in the state of Florida.

In May 1999, I, as president of the American Beach Property Owners' Association, and others accepted a meritorious achievement award at the University of Florida, in Gainesville, Florida, on behalf of the community from the Florida Trust for Historic Preservation. The Florida Trust selected American Beach in recognition of its community accomplishments and significant contributions to the preservation of Florida's historic resources.

Marsha Dean Phelts was given an award in the Education/Media category for her 1997 published book, *An American Beach for African Americans.*

MaVynee Betsch,* known as the "Beach Lady," was a known outspoken voice and took solitary stands in speaking out and being recognized, wherever she could generating public exposure for American Beach.

Although American Beach has now become a senior citizen and past her three score and ten, she continues to live on!

---

* In 2002, MaVynee Betsch made public her plight with stomach cancer. "The Beach Lady," who was dubbed by outsiders as the icon of American Beach, passed away during the processing of this first publication. She was unique in character and had an extraordinary dedication for American Beach and the environment. She fought to protect American Beach from encroaching development. With her age running parallel to the age of American Beach, MaVynee's birth year was known to be the same year American Beach was founded in 1935. She passed away on Labor Day, September 5, 2005. Labor Day has been the historic and traditional closing of the beach for the summer season.

The community prepares for the Amelia Island-Fernandina Beach-Yulee Chamber of Commerce Third Thursday Network (Business After Hours), hosted by the American Beach Property Owners' Association, at the home (oceanside entrance) of Edna Calhoun on October 17, 1996.

James Robinson - October 17, 1996

Fernandina Beach News-Leader - May 1, 1996

A crowd gathers at American Beach on a Sunday afternoon in an effort to bring American Beach back to its heyday.

Chamber guests gather for Business After Hours at the (westside entrance) home of Edna Calhoun on Waldron Street. Edna was a Howard University retiree and Dean of Girls during my years at Florida A & M University in Tallahassee, Florida.

James Robinson - October 17, 1996

The Honorable Emmitt G. Coakley of the Nassau County Zoning Board was the facilitator-speaker for the "Building Our Community" orientation/reception held at the Ritz-Carlton.

Residents attend an American Beach workshop at the Ritz-Carlton.

James Robinson - April 19,1997

Participants attending an American Beach workshop at the Ritz-Carlton.

Residents had a chance to communicate at the opening night of the "Building Our Community" orientation/reception held at the Ritz-Carlton at Amelia Island. Program chairlady, Gladys Foster, far left. President Annette Myers welcomes the group.

James Robinson - April 19, 1997

James Robinson - April 19, 1997

American Beach residents attending the Ritz-Carlton workshop.

James Robinson - April 19, 1997

American Beach residents attending the Ritz-Carlton workshop.   James Robinson - April 19, 1997

Property owners express their views at "American Beach Now and in the Future" workshop held at the Airport Holiday Inn at Jacksonville.

James Robinson - May 19, 1997

James Robinson - June 21, 1997

Nassau County governmental officials Sheriff Ray Geiger, Attorney Michael Mullen, Chairman Commissioner John Crawford, and County Coordinator Walt Gossett participated in the American Beach workshop. Missing from the photo was Nassau County Property Appraiser James Page.

Following the workshop with government officials, property owners meet to dine together at the 1878 Steakhouse in downtown historic Fernandina Beach.

James Robinson - June 21, 1997

"Association to Association" meeting in Jacksonville.   James Robinson - August 2, 1997
Long-time owners and cornerstones of American Beach wait for workshop to begin.

Residents met with another community group in Jacksonville for an "Association to Association" workshop, held at the Red Lobster Restaurant.
                                                                          James Robinson - August 2, 1997

James Robinson - 1997

Annette Myers, MaVynee Betsch "Beach Lady," the great-granddaughter of A.L. Lewis, and News-Leader correspondent pose for a photo at the "Association to Association" workshop in Jacksonville, Florida, before heading home on our chartered bus. The bus was chartered from Benjamin's Cab and Coach Service of Fernandina Beach.

Association to Association Workshop, August 2, 1997. Photographer James Robinson, Ethel McClenton, and the Harrises on the right.

Community participates in the Isle of Eight Flags Shrimp Festival in the historic district of downtown Fernandina Beach. The movie "Sunshine State" filmed at American Beach, and on Amelia Island, included a pirate festival scene.

James Robinson - May 1998

Flowers sent to the American Beach Association from Kuhn Flowers, for Folio Weekly, *for our Beautification Enhancement Project, and other community accomplishments.*

James Robinson - November 17, 1998

Marsha Phelts, Annette Myers, and association grant writer Ruth Waters McKay after accepting the Florida Preservation Awards for American Beach meritorious organizational achievements at the University of Florida in Gainesville, Florida, and for the preservation of Florida's historic resources.

Michael Phelts - May 20, 1999

"Each generation goes further than the generation preceding it because it stands on the shoulders of that generation."

(Ronald Reagan)

"Most leaders are indispensable, but to produce a major social change, many ordinary people must also be involved."

(Anne Firor Scott)

Chapter 11

Passing the Torch

Upon the 75th anniversary of American Beach in 2010, the community and Nassau County have come a long way in perpetuating the history of the American Beach enclave.

Monday, February 19, 2007, marked an observance of the American Beach Property Owners' Association Presidents' Day.[1] This was in recognition of all presidents who assumed responsibility in giving leadership to the preservation of the American Beach community.

This book would not be complete without a profile of each prestigious leader who carried the torch from one passing of time to the next. All of these leaders saw a need to do what they were led to do with the help of others in their own space and time.

HISTORIC AMERICAN BEACH

A.B.P.O.A. Presidents
"Past and Present"

Ben Durham
1982-1986

Frank Morgan
1986-1988

Bobby Dollison
1988-1990

Henry Adams
1990-1992

Annette Myers
1992-2001

Henry Adams
2001-2005

Carlton Jones
2005-present

American Beach Property Owners Association

Willie B. Evans, Jr.
Unchartered President
American Beach Homeowner Association
1967 and continuous to 1980

Mr. Evans, who was the owner of Evans' Rendezvous, sensed a need for organization after the decline of American Beach in the 1960s. Because of his prominent business ventures, good looks, tall stature, overall well-groomed appearance, and involvement in the Fernandina Beach community, there was no question about following his direction and his concern for the welfare of American Beach. He was the owner of Evans' Rendezvous (bar and restaurant) from 1948 to 1980. In 1980, the business we often called the bar, the club, or the liquor store, was sold to high school coach William J. Weathersbee of Jacksonville, Florida. Evans, as he was called, was the man of American Beach and around town. His name was a household word throughout the Fernandina area.

Operating his business, which also included a club out on nearby Highway A1A, was encouragement to others to open businesses in the area for everyone to enjoy.

The Ocean Rendezvous, renamed by Coach Weathersbee, is still standing today and waiting in the shadows to be restored. It will always be remembered as the club that hosted many big time famous entertainers such as Cab Calloway, Duke Ellington and Ray Charles.

Willie Evans lived in his two-story apartment adjacent to the bar and restaurant.

He passed away in Jacksonville, Florida, in 1996.[2]

Ben Durham, Jr.
Founding Charter President
American Beach, Inc.
1982 - 1986

Ben Durham was an outstanding educator and businessman from Jacksonville, Florida. When the opportunity presented itself during his adulthood, he jumped at the opportunity to purchase property near the ocean. He built his oceanfront vacation home on the south end of Gregg Street. He encouraged family members and others to build homes or to purchase property and vacation on American Beach as well.

His interest in American Beach stemmed from memories of his childhood days of coming to the beach with his parents.

From his concern for the revitalization and perpetuation of the community, the need for organization and preservation of American Beach was without question. The community became involved as well as citizens from the Fernandina Beach area, because this was the only beach they knew. Under his leadership, the American Beach Association, Inc., was founded and issued a charter from the State of Florida on February 26, 1982. Meetings were held in the A.L. Lewis Motel.

The Board of Directors were: Ben Durham, Jr., President; Frank Morgan, Sr., Vice-President; and Myrtis C. Thomas, Secretary. Serving as Trustees were Dr. Elizabeth Jones, Maxcell Wilson, Mrs. I. E. Williams, and Leroy Tyler from Fernandina. Elmo Myers (my husband) and I were charter members of this organization.

State of Florida

Department of State

I certify that the attached is a true and correct copy of the Articles of Incorporation of

AMERICAN BEACH, INC.

filed on February 26, 1982.

The Charter Number for this corporation is 762126.

Given under my hand and the
Great Seal of the State of Florida,
at Tallahassee, the Capital, this the
26th   day of February 1982.

George Firestone
Secretary of State

CORP 104 Rev. 6-79

ARTICLES OF INCORPORATION   FILED

The undersigned, acting as Incorporator(s) of a corporation under

the Florida General Corporation Act, adopt(s) the following Articles of

Incorporation for such corporation:

   1. NAME. The name of this corporation is AMERICAN BEACH, INC.,

      a non-profit organization.

   2. DURATION. The period of its duration is perpetual.

   3. PURPOSE. The general nature of the business to be transacted

by this corporation is: The redevelopment of American Beach and engage in

any activities or business permitted under the laws of the United States

and Florida.

   4. CAPITAL STOCK: Corporation authorized no stock.

   5. INITIAL REGISTERED OFFICE AND AGENT. The name and address of the

initial registered agent and office of this corporation is as follows:

      Mr. Ben Durham
      3839 Stuart Street
      Jacksonville, Florida 32209

   6. INITIAL BOARD OF DIRECTORS. This corporation shall have six

directors initially. The number of directors may be either increased or

decreased from time to time by an amendment of the bylaws of the corpora-

tion in a manner provided by law, but shall never be less than five.

   The names and addresses of the initial directors of this corporation

are:

Mr. Ben Durham - President 3839 Stuart Street Jacksonville, Florida 32209	Mr. Maxcell Wilson P. O. Box 151 Fernandina Beach, Florida 32034
Dr. Elizabeth Jones 828 West 31st Street Jacksonville, Florida 32209	Mrs. I. E. Williams - Treasurer 2827 Ribault Scenic Drive Jacksonville, Florida 32208
Mrs. Myrtis C. Thomas - Secretary 4326 Jerome Avenue Jacksonville, Florida 32209	Mr. Leroy Tyler 8275 7th Avenue Fernandina Beach, Florida 32034

   7. INCORPORATOR(s) The names and address(es) of the Incorporator(s)

signing these articles of Incorporation (is(are):

      Mr. Ben Durham
      3839 Stuart Street
      Jacksonville, Florida 32209

      Dr. Elizabeth Jones
      828 West 31st Street
      Jacksonville, Florida 32209

      Mrs. Myrtis C. Thomas
      4326 Jerome Avenue
      Jacksonville, Florida 32209

8. QUALIFICATION OF MEMBERS AND MANNER OF ADMISSION. The officers of the corporation shall consist of a president, a vice-president, a secretary, a financial secretary and a treasurer, who shall be elected for one year by the property owners of American Beach at the first meeting after the annual meeting on January 15 of each year of the property owners, and who shall hold office until their successors are elected and qualify.

9. MANAGEMENT OF AFFAIRS. The Board of Directors shall have the power and authority to fill any vacancies in office arising from resignation, death or otherwise, to be filled by the Board of Directors at any regular or special meeting. They shall have the power to manager affair in such manners as are usually imposed upon such officials of corporations and as are required by law.

10. BY-LAWS - HOW MADE AND AMENDED. The By-Laws may be amended or repealed, or new By-Laws many be made and adopted at any annual or special meeting of members (property owners) called for the purpose, by the vote or written assent of the members representing a majority (2/3) vote.

11. AMENDMENTS OF ARTICLES. This corporation reserves the right to amend or repeal any provisions contained in these Articles of Incorporation, or any amendment hereto, and any right conferred upon the members is subject to this reservation.

IN WITNESS WHEREOF, the undersigned Incorporator(s) has/have executed the foregoing Articles of Incorporation, and (he) (they) acknowledged to and before me that (he) (they) executed such instrument this _26 th_ day of _Feb_, 19 _22_

Myrtis C. Thomas

Ben Durham Jr.

Elizabeth B. Jones

STATE OF FLORIDA
COUNTY OF DUVAL

BEFORE ME, the undersigned authority, personally appeared Ben Durham, Myrtis Thomas and Elizabeth Jones to be known to be the persons who executed the foregoong Articles of Incorporation, and (he) (they) acknowledged to and before me that (he) (they) executed such instrument.

IN WITNESS WHEREOF, I have hereunto set my hand and seal this _26 th_ day of February, 19 _22_.

Ernest R. Thomas

NOTARY PUBLIC, STATE OF FLORIDA

Notary Public, State of Florida at Large
My Commission Expires Feb. 25, 1984
Bonded Thru Troy Fain Insurance Inc.

Frank Morgan, Sr.
President
American Beach, Inc.
1986 – 1988

Frank Morgan, Sr. and his wife Emma Morgan, who lived in Jacksonville, Florida, acquired and owned an oceanfront home on American Beach they called "Los Angeles." They were members of the chartered organization in 1982 and dedicated to the preservation of American Beach. When Mr. Durham could no longer serve as president due to ill health and when he passed away in 1986, Frank Morgan, Sr., became president. Meetings continued to be held in the lobby of the historic A.L. Lewis Motel.

Mrs. Morgan was an invaluable helpmate to her husband. She saw that refreshments were available at every meeting. She served as chair of the Government-Liaison Committee and kept the association well informed. She proudly created and distributed to members an alphabetical resource directory consisting of property owners, telephone numbers, addresses, Nassau County resources, important contacts and other valuable information.

Mrs. Morgan's never-ending resounding slogan was "Let's Save American Beach."

Mr. Morgan advocated a lighted community by encouraging everyone to invest in streetlights for a safer community. Under his leadership, dumpsters and portable toilets were placed, by the county, near the Lewis Street beach access for community and public use.

Through the years, the Morgans acquired the most property in the area. They were owners of the large parking lot facing Evans' Rendezvous at the corner of Gregg and Lewis Street where hundreds of visitors parked their vehicles on weekends. Their son, Frank Morgan, Jr. assisted them in this business venture.

The Morgan family, including their son Frank, Jr., were American Beach ambassadors to many African-Americans by encouraging them to buy properties and to vacation on historic American Beach. In the late 1900s, Frank Morgan, Jr., became a Nassau County Realtor to help in this endeavor.

Bobby Dollison
President
American Beach, Inc.
1988 – 1990

Bobby Dollison is the acquired owner and operater of the historic A.L. Lewis Motel and the American Beach public water system.

Over the years, the water system known as the historic well, located on the historic motel property, has been a valuable water supply system for residents of the community.

Judge Henry Lee Adams, Jr.
President
American Beach, Inc.
1990 –1992

In 1993, the Honorable Henry Lee Adams, Jr., of Jacksonville, Florida was assigned to a judicial vacancy in the Tampa, Florida, Division of the United States District Court, Middle District of Florida.

This appointment ended his two-year term of office as president of American Beach, Inc.

In 1991, minor amendment changes were made to the association by-laws. Meetings were held in the Franklintown Church.

Annette McCollough Myers
President
American Beach, Inc.
1992 – 1996

President
American Beach Property Owners' Association, Inc.
1996 – 2001

Annette McCollough Myers was the fifth president of the founding American Beach, Inc., chartered association. Annette is home-grown, born and reared in Fernandina, and graduated from the all-black Peck High School in Fernandina Beach. Growing up, she enjoyed summer visits to American Beach with family, church and community groups. In later years, Elmo Myers and Annette spent courtship times on American Beach enjoying great home-cooked seafood and listening to the oldies of the 1950s. The Myers purchased Ms. Lottie's place on Ervin Street in the 1960s. Today, it is listed in the National Registry of Historic Places and continues to be maintained. Named for its original owner, it is called Martha's Hideaway.

Elmo and Annette Myers were members of the first organization under Willie B. Evans and members of the first chartered organization in 1982.

Annette's leadership began in 1991 as vice-president of American Beach, Inc., and she has given over a decade of service to the American Beach community. She has been the longest serving president, the first and only female president and earned the name *Madam President* in association meetings. She was considered by many to be most effective, consistent and persistent in her administration for getting things done. She has worked with county officials on many levels.

In 1996, she led in revamping the association's charter and by-laws. The community's chartered forum was renamed the American Beach Property Owners' Association, Inc., and continues under that name to this day. Renaming the association was a big boost and helped in obtaining community grants.

Her administration was forthright in keeping development from destroying American Beach. Much was done to preserve the historic legacy and integrity of American Beach and to ward off big-time development including high rises and condos.

Among the significant accomplishments under the Myers administration were: continuation and participation in the Isle of Eight Flags Shrimp Festival that started around 1990, landscaping, palm tree planting, front-door entrance signs, beach walkovers and wheelchair accessibility at Burney Park, street paving, grant writing, first community center ground-breaking on May 2000, homeowner beautification award programs, removal of abandoned and derelict buildings, sidewalks, quarterly newsletters to property owners, neigborhood Safety Patrol program, grant funded Building Our Community work-shops, neighborhood clean-up days in cooperation with Keep Nassau Beautiful, pump station installed by the county at Lewis Street and Ocean Boulevard to improve rainwater drainage, widening of Lewis Street from Mary Avenue to Ocean Boulevard, and first Founders Day program in 1995. Community garbage and debris street dumping was eliminated. Property owners now contract for private pick-up services. In 1999, an American Beach sign was installed at the entrance of Burney Road and AIA compliments of Osprey Village at Amelia Island Plantation.

Of particular interest was the arduous task of preparation and documentation for the listing of American Beach on the National Register of Historic Places. On May 20, 2000, the Florida Historic Marker for American Beach was sited on Lewis Street, the main thoroughfare.

Annette Myers, a retired educator, community activist, and author, continues to make significant contributions to the American Beach community through her writings and participation in community affairs. Her husband passed away in 1987. She continues to live in *Martha's Hideaway*, and her historic palatial home is shared on special occasions with family, friends, and for other special events. The home has also served as a complimentary bed-and-breakfast accommodation, for several visitors to the island.

Mission Statement

The mission of the American Beach Property Owners' Association is to continue the tradition established by the founders of American Beach (1935) and, its parent organization, American Beach, Inc. (1982) by working to ensure the general welfare and safety of the American Beach enclave and its residents. Further, the founding purpose of the American Beach Property Owners' Association, Inc. (1996) is to create a healthy community for property owners socially, economically, and aesthetically—and to do such other things as are enunciated by the membership of the Association and its Board of Trustees for the good of the community.

Judge Henry Lee Adams, Jr.
President
American Beach Property Owners' Association, Inc.
2001 - 2005

The year 2000 brought Judge Adams to an appointment back home in Jacksonville, where he was assigned to the Jacksonville Division of Florida. In 2001, he became president once again at American Beach, where he previously served in 1990-92.

In 1991, Judge Adams took pictures of numerous abandoned and hazardous buildings. This was an effort to clean up the community and to contact property owners about those properties that were eyesores in the community.

He is an advocate for water and sewer services. In July of 1991, an American Beach delegation traveled to Washington, D. C., to seek federal assistance to help with the development, preservation, and enhancement of this northeast Florida Coastal African-American community.

On December 18, 1993, American Beach, Inc., under Myers' leadership, sponsored a banquet in Judge Adams' honor for all his judicial accomplishments. This first-class affair was held at the Ritz-Carlton Hotel on Amelia Island. The banquet was well attended by the American Beach community, friends and colleagues, Duval County and the Nassau County community.

The Judge maintains his activism in the association.

Judge Adams and his wife Elaine, with other family members enjoy their newly renovated home on American Beach overlooking the Atlantic Ocean.

Dr. Carlton D. Jones
President
American Beach Property Owners' Association, Inc.
2005 – January, 2011

Carlton D. Jones is quick to give praises and honor to those who served before his time and to those who helped carry the torch to where we are today. He gives credit to his board members, shareholders of American Beach and others who have helped in the preservation of historic American Beach. He has served and represented American Beach in many ways and works with officials and others on many levels in Nassau County and Duval County. Rev. Jones is an associate pastor at Bethel Baptist Church in Jacksonville, Florida.

He is an outstanding business man and his involvements are many.

He serves as president of the Renaissance Design Build Group of Jacksonville, Inc. and Renaissance Downtown Development, Inc., and Chairman of the Renaissance Group of Americans, LLC. He is involved with other professional and business groups as well.

Under his leadership, American Beach has a website. On March 30, 2010, a ribbon cutting was held for the American Beach Community Center and Museum. Finally, a beautiful building sits at the corner of Mary Avenue and Julia Street.

He has helped to finalize grant writing and funds have been received to begin restoration of Evans' Rendezvous.

Dr. Jones enjoys his spacious mansion-type home on American Beach with his wife Barbara, other family members and grandchildren.

Aware of his many obligations and time restraints, American Beach members and citizens are thankful for his leadership and his spirituality.

"People from all over the world visit American
Beach because it is sacred."

(MaVynee Betsch)

Chapter 12

An American Beach Icon
"The Beach Lady"

MaVynee Betsch was the great-granddaughter of Abraham Lincoln
Lewis. Documented records, of the Kingsley family line, show that
MaVynee (Sammis-Lewis) Betsch was a descendent of Zephaniah and
Anna Kingsley of Kingsley Plantation.[1]

She was born in Jacksonville, Florida, on January 13, 1935, the
same year and month American Beach was founded. She was the
eldest of three children born to John Thomas Betsch, Sr., and Mary
Frances (Sammis) Lewis Betsch.[2]

She attended public schools in Jacksonville and Washington, D.C.,
and a well-established all girls middle and high school private Methodist
school, Boylan Haven in Jacksonville.[3]

After graduation in 1951, and then studying in Europe and
Germany, she returned to Jacksonville in 1962 to study conservation
and the environment. She moved to American Beach, founded under
her great-grandfather's leadership, around 1977 and homesteaded on
property owned by others.

Because of her colorful lifestyle, striking appearance, wit, humor
and eccentricity, MaVynee was called the icon of American Beach, a
free and civic spirit who could get by with anything that came out of her
mouth for the preservation of American Beach and the environment.

MaVynee was an environmentalist, whose interest was the land,
ocean, and air.

She often called American Beach a "one of a kind" enclave
and referred to up-scale look-alike, private, and exclusive gated

developments as HUD housing for rich folks.[4]

The Beach Lady, who proclaimed herself the unofficial mayor of American Beach, died of stomach cancer on the morning of, Labor Day, September 5, 2005. This day has always been the traditional closing of the beach for the summer season.

MaVynee Betsch Commentary[5]
For the *Fernandina Beach News-Leader*
February 28, 2003

"NaNa, American Beach dune, lifts us to spiritual heights."

Greetings from American Beach, the only African-American [beachfront] community in Florida. Greetings also from NaNa (West African Twi for Grandmother), which is the tallest sand dune on our island and beloved by all at American Beach who feel a spiritual high just being near her sacred presence.

My name is MaVynee Oshun Betsch and I was born in 1935, the year of the "Great Hurricane." Oldtimers in south Florida still speak of the unusual flecks of light on the sand dunes—so alive with electricity was that powerful storm.

Sand dunes and sand in general have always had a special magic for me. My fondest childhood memories are of making mud pies after an afternoon rain. [The] softness in my hands seemed somehow loving, playful—and mosquito bites less annoying upon receiving a mud pack!

Summer vacations from college were anticipated with happiness, for it meant trips to the beach and sand castle building. My dream world of sand even followed me to Europe, where I sang opera in Germany. My first role was Salome by Richard Strauss, which takes place in the Middle East with a desert sand dune background.

Some years later, my grandfather and mother passed and I went to live in his house at American Beach. I was in paradise at last—the view of NaNa to the southwest and dunes to the east with hours on end of enjoying the sound and play of wind as nature's sand artist!

My great-grandfather was one of seven founders of the Afro-

American Life Insurance Co. in 1901….He helped the Afro acquire the land in the '30s as blacks could not use the "whites only" beach.

Mother Nature's sand was for him the Great Healer. As children, we would dig a large hole in the wet beach sand, bury his right side with the arthritis pain and let the sea salts and warmth of the sun bring him comfort.

Climbing the big sand dune to meditate at the top is my religion. As my feet sink into her softness, somehow, from up there, all my worries seem to vanish.

Animals and sand open up fascinating ideas for poetic thought– dry sand baths of birds and wet sand baths for Namibian elephants, my favorite African animal because the female is the leader and she is a vegetarian.

My other favorite is the gopher tortoise, which digs a home in the sand dune and shares it with 80 other critters! ….

Watching the worker ants on the dunes suggest a philosophical meaning– again females! The lowly oyster secretes the substance for the beauty of the pearl in response to irritation from sand entering its shell.

I share my 6-foot height with the sea oats, that elegant plant with roots that embraces the sand, thus allowing the wind to build higher dunes where one may watch the beautiful moon rise over the ocean.

Death will not take me from my beloved NaNa. I wish my ashes to be part of that eternal softness of sand—a magic world that makes my life a constant joy at American Beach, my sacred place!

Beach Lady Thoughts and Sayings

"I believe in reincarnation, and I hope to come back (to earth) as a butterfly."

"Humans are too boring, never again."

From the answering machine…"If you are getting this message, I have transformed myself into a butterfly, flitting about American Beach, taking nectar from wild flowers and immersing myself in her environment."

"When you look across the ocean from American Beach, the next continent you see is Africa."

"The less you have on the inside, the more you have on the outside." A quote from her great-grandfather.

"Getting the most from the least and living peacefully in harmony with nature is the most rewarding lifestyle."

For more on the "Beach Lady," see *The Big Sand Dune and The Beach Lady,* book by Annette McCollough Myers. Also visit www.missmarthashideaway.com or www.highpitchedhum.net.

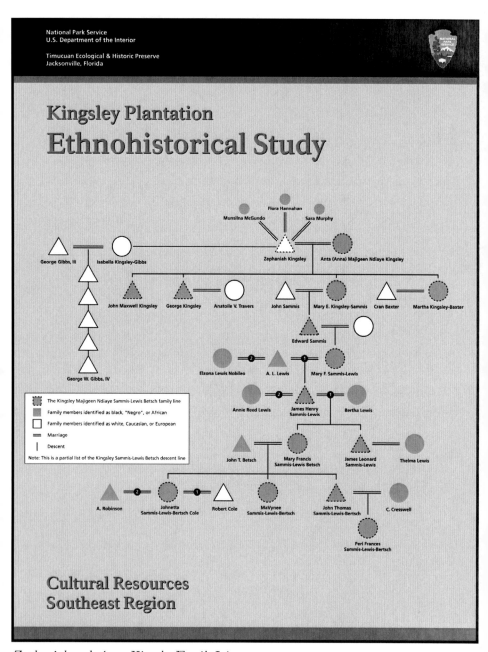

Zephaniah and Anna Kingsley Family Line.
http://www.nps.gov/history/history/online_books/timu/timu_ethno.pdf

Wedding portrait of Ferdinand "Fernando" Charles Suhrer.
Wedding portrait of Eva Rosa Plotts Suhrer.

Andrew B, Suhrer. The great-grandson of Ferdinand Charles Suhrer.

"Each age, it is found, must write its own books; or rather, each generation for the next succeeding."

(Ralph Waldo Emerson)

Chapter 13

Face to Face with History

Ferdinand "Fernando" Charles Suhrer
(Born October 18, 1837 – Died February 8, 1884)

Life brings twists, and on Amelia Island in 2010, I had the rare pleasure of meeting and becoming a friend of Andrew B. Suhrer, the great-grandson of Ferdinand C. Suhrer. In the 1800s, Ferdinand Suhrer once owned American Beach land called the Suhrer Tract. He was a native of the Grand Duchy of Baden, Germany. In 1856, he immigrated to America and studied medicine until the American Civil War broke out. On August 13, 1862, he enlisted in the Union Army as a private in the 107th Ohio Volunteer Infantry and quickly rose to the rank of major. When the war ended in 1865, Major Suhrer married his longtime sweetheart to whom he was engaged, Eva Rosa Plotts of Norwalk, Ohio.

During military assignments to various places and sites such as Fort Clinch, and the beautiful beaches in Fernandina, Suhrer fell in love with Fernandina. Through correspondence with a businessman acquaintance, he was offered work at one of the area hotels. Several months later, he and his new bride moved to Fernandina.

Suhrer lived the life of a prominent citizen and respected gentleman in Fernandina. Through civic, political and other held positions, he became widely known throughout Nassau County.

While serving as tax collector in 1874-1875, Fernando purchased an entire beachfront property for $6.75 at a property auction sale due to delinquent property taxes. This land would one day become a "Negro Ocean Playground."

While serving as President of the City Council, Fernando Suhrer was also manager of a popular hotel in downtown Fernandina for railroad workers and tourist,s called the Mansion House Hotel. The hotel was located on the right corner of 3rd Street, two blocks north of Centre Street. On February 8, 1884, he was shot and fatally wounded on the porch steps of the Mansion House by Thomas Jefferson (T.J.) Eppes, Jr. Eppes was a Mansion boarder and a conductor on the Florida Transit and Peninsular Railroad.

The murderer, Thomas Jefferson Eppes, Jr., was the great-grandson of President Thomas Jefferson.

Years after Fernando's tragic death, Eva Suhrer, a widow left with the rearing of six children, was in need of money. She, therefore, sold the ocean-front property to another land buyer for a hefty $800. Over time, the Pension Bureau of the Afro-American Life Insurance Company purchased portions of this same land to start American Beach. The first of three parcels was purchased in 1935 for $2,000.

Eva and Fernando are buried together in the historic Bosque Bello Cemetery in Fernandina.

Andy B. Suhrer was in Fernandina Beach for the 2010 Amelia Island Book Festival. Both he and I were selected authors for the book fair. I was introduced to Andy at the Books Plus bookstore by Maggie Carter-de Vries who is the new owner of Books Plus in Fernandina. Maggie is the author of *Amelia's Secrets*. Andy's book is called *The Flying Dutchmen*. Both their books are linked to F. C. Suhrer and his connection with the land now called historic American Beach.

Andy, of Dutch descent and a family man with three children, was born in Long Beach, California. He now lives in Coos Bay, Oregon, with his wife Mary Jo.

I find that history may not always repeat itself, but it has a strange way of coming back around in different ways and forms.

Commentaries

On Martha Hippard's Hideaway: "It is not often we find places of interest owned by African-Americans on the National Register of Historic Places. Many of our places in past history were burned, bought up by other people and destroyed or, for other reasons, no longer exist."
Dr. Ann Harris Stoddard
St. Marys, Georgia
Retired professor, University of North Florida, Jacksonville
Myers' Hideaway Celebration February 23, 2002.

On the Black Heritage Trail: "American Beach is certainly worthy of being recognized due to its historical significance."
Joseph Taylor, *Florida African-American Study Commission member and associate professor - Bethune Cookman College, Daytona Beach, Florida.*
Manley, Lisa. "American Beach could be earning its place in history." *Fernandina Beach News-Leader, June 26, 1991, A8.*

"No one at American Beach should fear harmful effects from the plantation (Amelia Island Plantation/AIP)." "We've always tried to be good neighbors in working with them."
Jack Healan, *AIP president and CEO.*
Kinner, Derek L. "Amelia golf, homes on tap/American Beach gets Amelia project concessions." *Florida Times-Union, March 13, 1997, B1.*

"Development is not our problem. We're our own worst enemy."
Annette Myers, *ABPOA president.*
Sharp, Deborah . "Waves of change beat upon our community." *USA Today, July 21, 1998, A6.*

"The city of Miami is currently debating whether or not to create its own version of North Florida's American Beach, Virginia Key Beach, into a living Civil Rights Memorial in honor of those African-Americans who tirelessly fought for equality here in South Florida versus the possibility of handing the island over to a private developer for a commercial like site. The struggle that my family and friends are waging to save American Beach is symbolic of what African-Americans are experiencing in Miami-Dade County, for if we do not succeed in both fronts, we will not only NOT have a place to fish, we will have no fishermen either."

Barbara M. Carey-Shuler, Ed.D., *Miami-Dade County Commissioner Assistant superintendent-Dade County Public Schools 1995.*

Carey-Shuler, Barbara. "No Day at the Beach." *South Florida Newsweek, April 22-28, 1999, 6.*

"I applaud the County Commission's efforts that they recognize the importance of preserving Nassau County for residents, future generations and visitors."

Regina Duncan, *president, Amelia Island-Fernandina Beach-Yulee Chamber of Commerce.*

Schaefers, Allison. "Nassau establishes panel to catalog historic places." *Florida Times-Union/Nassau Neighbors, March 16, 2002, 4.*

"Maybe a taste of the 1960s was in order this time. And maybe after it's all over, the people causing the problems will realize that, during a time when public beach-front is shrinking, respect is a small price to pay to save one of the nation's last stretches of beach created with African-Americans in mind."

Tonyaa Weathersbee, *Florida Times-Union columnist, Jacksonville, Florida.*

Weathersbee, Tonyaa. Viewpoint: "Respect is a small price blacks must pay to save American Beach." *Florida Times-Union, May 25, 1998, A19.*

"Martha's Hideaway is an important piece of history as it is reflective of one of the historical remnants of this historical coastal community and has a story all of its own. It is important to preserve each individual element to maintain an overall harmony of distinction. The loss of familiar surroundings disrupts the sense of continuity in community life and contributes to feelings of personal, social, and civic disorder." March 18, 2005.

> Maggie McCollough Carey, Ph.D. (personal interview)
> *Retired educator and superintendent*
> *Gary, Indiana School System*

"This [American Beach] is not a blighted area."

> Commissioner Marianne Ann Marshall
> *Nassau County Commission Meeting*
> *February 9, 2004*

"American Beach is a jewel worth polishing and saving." "There is a heritage there, a culture and a richness not found in other places."

> John Crawford, *Nassau County Commissioner (1998)*
> Clary, Mike. "Preservationist cherish beach's black heritage." *Los Angeles Times, September 24, 1998, A5.*

"We all want to preserve the heritage and character...And the best way to do that is for folks to invest in property here and then care for it."

> Annette Myers, *president, American Beach Property Owners' Association.*
> Clary, Mike. "Preservationist cherish beach's black heritage." *Los Angeles Times, September 24, 1998, A5.*

"Congratulations on the listing of your home on the National Register of Historic Places. You have a beautiful home and history will reflect that you have been a worthy and appreciative caretaker." February 2002.

> Bobby Dollison and Diane (personal correspondence)
> *Owner, American Beach Villas, formerly A.L. Lewis Motel, American Beach.*

"Franklin Town existed for over 100 years. If history repeats itself, American Beach is good for about 100 years also."

Marsha Dean Phelts, *author, An American Beach for African Americans.*

Martin, Kimberly N. "Ghost Town." *Folio Weekly, August 25, 1998.*

"Congratulations on getting Martha Hippard's Hideaway officially listed on the National Register of Historic Places. We have long admired your commitment and dedication to American Beach. This historic celebration is indeed a reflection of your vision and perseverance in keeping the American Beach experience alive." February 23, 2002.

Tony and Lawanda Brown (personal correspondence)
American Beach

"American Beach is a peaceful and quiet pristine kind of historical seaside community, unlike other places I have seen and visited." April 22, 2005.

Curtis B. Davis (personal interview)
Owner, Cable LLC
Gary, Indiana

Dear Annette.... "It has certainly been my pleasure to work with you over the years.... A great deal has been accomplished during your tenure as president." January 22, 2001.

Michael S. Mullen (personal correspondence)
Nassau County Attorney

"All things are subject to change, and we change with them."
—*Anonymous*

Afterword

Since the 1960s, although shrinking in size, American Beach has been a community of continuous improvements.

In the face of much adversity and publicity, we are a community that remembers yesterday, striving today, and always facing the challenges and existence of this tiny enclave.

American Beach, as it was, is a remnant and legacy of days gone past. It is a historical monument and landmark of African-American history on the east coast of Florida. It is the only remaining African- American coastal community in the state. This history of African-American life as it existed needs to be perpetuated and protected from undesirable and incompatible development, as the founders would have it.

American Beach is unique in several ways in that it still exists much as it did 70-some years ago--pristine and pretty much undeveloped. Over the years, many families have continued to hold on to their properties despite the threat of encroaching development. The community has grown to become overwhelmingly a single-family residential neighborhood. Little by little, more families are living at American Beach year round. Residents have also become more cognizant and appreciative of the community's 2002 listing on the National Register of Historic Places.

The community has stood the test of time through the help and concerns of many, including property owners, residents, Department of State, various members of the Nassau County community of individuals, organizations, corporations, governmental officials, and others, who have made substantial contributions to the American Beach community through the years and during my years of service. Likewise, there are those individuals of American Beach who have made remarkable accomplishments that contribute greatly toward the history and perpetuation of Historic American Beach.

Salutations go to the founders of the Afro-American Life Insurance Company and its Pension Bureau under the leadership of Dr. A.L. Lewis for the vision to create an African-American Coastal Resort Community, Willie B. Evans—the first American Beach Homeowners President, to Ben Durham—the first American Beach, Incorporated President, and other community leaders who are passionate about its history and legacy.

Appendix

Relevant Documents
Property Owners List

Collection of the Author – Florida Black Heritage Trail postcard. Ree-Olyd Souvenirs.

State of Florida

THIS IS TO CERTIFY THAT
IN RECOGNITION OF ITS HISTORIC SIGNIFICANCE

The Hippard House

HAS BEEN OFFICIALLY LISTED IN

The National Register of Historic Places

EFFECTIVE

The Twelfth Day of October, Two Thousand One

BY THE
NATIONAL PARK SERVICE, DEPARTMENT OF THE INTERIOR
WASHINGTON, D.C.

Katherine Harris
SECRETARY OF STATE

Janet Snyder Matthews
STATE HISTORIC PRESERVATION OFFICER

State of Florida

THIS IS TO CERTIFY THAT
IN RECOGNITION OF ITS HISTORIC SIGNIFICANCE

American Beach Historic District

HAS BEEN OFFICIALLY LISTED IN

The National Register of Historic Places

EFFECTIVE

The Twenty-eighth Day of January Two Thousand Two

BY THE
NATIONAL PARK SERVICE, DEPARTMENT OF THE INTERIOR
WASHINGTON, D.C.

STATE HISTORIC PRESERVATION OFFICER

SECRETARY OF STATE

FLORIDA
.TRUST.
FOR HISTORIC
PRESERVATION

The Florida Trust
for Historic Preservation, Inc.
bestows this award
in recognition
of the significant achievement
in the preservation
of Florida's
rich Heritage.

Florida Preservation Award 1999

American Beach Property Owners' Association, Inc.

*In Recognition of Meritorious Organizational Achievement
in the field of Preservation*

President,
Florida Trust for Historic Preservation, Inc.

Awards Committee Chair

CONGRESS OF THE UNITED STATES OF AMERICA
HOUSE OF REPRESENTATIVES
WASHINGTON, D.C. 20515

CORRINE BROWN　　　　　　　　　　　　　　　　　　3RD DISTRICT, FLORIDA

MARTHA HIPPARD'S HIDEAWAY
COMMEMORATION

　　Today as we honor "Martha Hippard's Hideaway, it is evident how great God is! He has seen fit to place this house on the National Registry so that every citizen and visitor of American Beach can enjoy the grandeur and history of this majestic site.

　　As we reflect on the blessings, joy and happiness this house has been to the Myers family, I am proud to see the multi-faceted history of this structure honored by being placed on the National Registry.

　　This house has seen many times, many people, and many occasions. Many houses have not withstood the ravages and passage of time because of nature, neglect, and demolition. I am pleased that the contribution of the Myers family to American Beach is readily evident and stands as an historical site on this special day of commemoration!

　　With kindest regards, I am

　　　　　　　　　Sincerely,

　　　　　　　　　Corrine Brown
　　　　　　　　　Corrine Brown
　　　　　　　　　Member of Congress

CB:yr

RESOLUTION NO. 2002- 024

A RESOLUTION OF THE BOARD OF COUNTY COMMISSIONERS OF NASSAU COUNTY, FLORIDA, RECOGNIZING THE HISTORICAL AND CULTURAL SIGNIFICANCE OF THE PLACEMENT OF THE HOME OF MRS. ANNETTE MYERS AT AMERICAN BEACH ON THE NATIONAL REGISTER OF HISTORIC PLACES

WHEREAS, American Beach was founded in 1935 and is the first stop on Florida's Black Heritage Trail; and

WHEREAS, the "Hippard House", located at 5406 Ervin Street, American Beach, was built in 1938; and

WHEREAS, Mrs. Annette Myers purchased the home in 1961 and has maintained the historic significance of the residence; and

WHEREAS, the home of Mrs. Annette Myers is now listed on the National Register of Historic Places as of October 12, 2001.

NOW, THEREFORE, BE IT RESOLVED this 28th day of January, 2002 by the Board of County Commissioners of Nassau County, Florida, that:

Nassau County joins in celebrating the historical and cultural significance of Mrs. Annette Myers' home at American Beach, which now enriches all of historical Amelia Island and Nassau County, Florida.

BOARD OF COUNTY COMMISSIONERS
NASSAU COUNTY, FLORIDA

NICK D. DEONAS
Its: Chairman

_____ _____
DAVID C. HOWARD   VICKIE SAMUS

_____   _____
FLOYD L. VANZANT   MARIANNE MARSHALL

ATTEST:

_____
J. M. "CHIP" OXLEY, JR.
Its: Ex-Officio Clerk

Approved as to form by the
Nassau County Attorney:

_____
MICHAEL S. MULLIN

OFFICE OF:

Nassau County Property Appraiser

PHONES:
(904) 321-5733
JAX (904) 353-9821
HILLIARD - CALLAHAN
(904) 879-4227

JAMES PAGE, C.F.A., APPRAISER

P. O. BOX 870
11 N. 14th STREET, ROOM 6
FERNANDINA BEACH, FLORIDA 32034

December 12, 1995

Mrs. Annette Myers
P O Box 206
Fernandina Beach FL, 32035

Dear Mrs. Myers:

This letter will confirm our conversation this morning regarding future
assessments for American Beach properties.

Whatever development Amelia Island Plantation or Summer Beach
does will have no direct effect on the assessed value of properties
within the American Beach Subdivisions. American Beach will be
assessed on sales and development within the American Beach area.

I trust this will be sufficient information. If we can be of further service
please feel free to call on this office.

Sincerely,

JAMES PAGE C F A
Nassau County
Property Appraiser

JP:ias

DEED BOOK 165   PAGE 331

COVENANTS AND BLANKET RESTRICTIONS

UNIT ONE OF AMERICAN BEACH -- SECTION THREE

KNOW ALL MEN BY THESE PRESENTS:

THAT WHEREAS; The Afro-American Pension Bureau, a Florida

Corporation, is the owner in fee simple of the lands, particularly

described herein below in Paragraph 1, and it is desired by the said Afro-

American Pension Bureau, Incorporated, to impose certain covenants and

restrictions upon the said lands for the general welfare of the owners

thereof, presently and in the future, and to that end;

NOW, THEREFORE, The Afro-American Pension Bureau, Incorporated,

its successors and assigns do, hereby, declare and impose upon the said

land and upon each of the said lots, severally, the covenants and

restrictions hereinafter set forth in the Paragraphs Nos. 1 to 9, inclusive,

which said covenants and restrictions shall constitute covenants on the

part of the said Afro-American Pension Bureau, Incorporated, its

respective representatives, successors and assigns and all such

purchasers and grantees and all persons claiming under them from this

date to be faithfully abided by, kept and performed. Be it understood,

1

however, that Lots 1, 2 and 3 of Block 1 and Lots 1, 2, 3, 4, 5 and 11 of

Block 2 are, hereby, excepted from these covenants and restrictions, the

said covenants and restrictions being as follows, to-wit:

PARAGRAPH I

For point of reference commence at a permanent reference monument
located at the Southwesterly corner of Tract C. American Beach Section Three, according to plat
recorded in the public records of Nassau County, Florida, in Plat Book 2, Page 64, and run
North eighty-nine degrees, fifty-three minutes East (N.89° 53'E.) along the Southerly
boundary of said Tract C, a distance of Six hundred two and thirty-six hundredths (602.36)
feet to an iron pipe for point of beginning.

From the point of beginning thus described run North zero degrees, seven minutes West
(N.0°.07'W.) a distance of one hundred (100) feet to a point; run thence North forty degrees,
forty-vive minutes West (N.40°.45W.) a distance of Sixty-five and ninety-two hundredths
(65.92) feet to be a point; run thence North two degrees, thirty-eight minutes, twenty seconds
East (N.2°38'20" E.) a distance of five hundred eighty-four and eight tenths (584.80) feet to a
point; run thence North eighty-seven degrees, twenty-one minutes, forty seconds West (N.87°
21' 40"W.) a distance of one hundred (100) feet to a permanent reference monument; run
thence North two degrees, thirty-eight minutes, twenty seconds East (N.2°38' 20" E.) a
distance of three hundred fifty (350) feet to a permanent reference monument; run thence
South eighty-seven degrees twenty-one minutes forty seconds East (S.87°21' 40" E.) a distance
of one hundred (100) feet to a point; run thence North two degrees, thirty-eight minutes,
twenty seconds East (N.2°38' 20" E.) a distance of five hundred twenty- six and fifty-two
hundredths (526.52) feet to a permanent reference monument, located in the Northerly line of
Tract C aforementioned; run thence North eighty-nine degrees thirty-four minutes East (N.
89°34' E.) along the Northerly line of said Tract C, a distance of three hundred ten (310) feet
more or less to the point where the Northerly line of said Tract C is intersected by the Atlantic
Ocean; run thence in a Southerly direction down said Ocean a distance of sixteen hundred
thirteen (1613) feet more or less to the point where the Atlantic Ocean is intersected by the
Southerly line of Tract C aforementioned; run thence South eighty-nine degrees, fifty-three
minutes West (S.89° 53'W.) along the Southerly line of said Tract C, a distance of two hundred
fifty-five (255) feet more or less to the point of beginning.

Excepting from the land thus described that portion of Tract C, American Beach-Section
Three aforementioned, more particularly described as follows:

2

For point of reference commence at the permanent reference monument mentioned in the above description and described therein as being located in the Northerly line of said Tract C, and run North eighty-nine degrees, thirty-four minutes East (N. 89° 34'E.) along the Northerly line of said Tract C, a distance of one hundred seventy-five and forty-four hundredths (175.44) feet to a permanent reference monument; run thence Southerly along the arc of a curve concave to the West and having a radius of four hundred fifty (450) feet, a chord distance of fifty (50) feet to an iron pipe for point of beginning, the bearing of said chord being South two degrees, forty-five minutes West (S.2° 45' W.).

From the point of beginning thus described continue in a Southerly direction along the arc of the aforementioned curve, a chord distance of eighty-two and thirty-seven hundredths (82.37) feet to a point of reverse curvature, the bearing of said chord being South eleven degrees, eleven minutes West (S.11° 11' W.); run thence along the arc of a curve concave to the East and having a radius of four hundred forty-three and eighty-three hundredths (443.83) feet, a chord distance of nineteen and eighty-seven hundredths (19.87) feet to an iron pipe, the bearing of the aforementioned chord being South fifteen degrees, nine minutes West (S.15° 09' W.); run thence North eighty-nine degrees thirty-four minutes East (N. 89° 34' E.) parallel to the Northerly line of said Tract C, a distance of one hundred forty-five (145) feet more or less to the Atlantic Ocean run thence up said Ocean in a Northerly direction a distance of one hundred (100) feet more or less to a point which bears North eighty-nine degrees, thirty-four minutes East (N. 89° 34' E.) from the point of beginning; run thence South eighty-nine degrees, thirty-four minutes West (S. 89° 34' W.) parallel to the Northerly line of said Tract C, a distance of one hundred thirty (130) feet more or less, to the point of beginning; Recorded in Plat Book 3, Page 19, Public Records of Nassau County, Florida.

PARAGRAPH II

There shall not be constructed or suffered to be erected upon any part of the above described property, any dwelling house or other building at a cost less than $2500.00; such cost to be calculated upon the net cost of labor and material alone, estimated at current prices. Said $2500.00 shall include a Garage or other outer-house. In no event, however, shall there be but one outer-house built along with any building on each lot in said Subdivision.

Nothing herein shall be construed to prevent the developer or its agent from erecting or maintaining on any part of said land, owned by it, such commercial and display signs and such temporary structures as may be reasonably required by it for development and sale purposes.

PARAGRAPH III

The building lines of the several lots in said Subdivision shall be as follows:

(a) The Easterly building line of all lots located in Block 1 of said Subdivision shall be 15 ft. from and parallel with the transit line as shown on said Plat and no building or any part

3

of portion there of shall at any time be erected or placed upon the space between said building line and the approximate high water line as shown on said Plat; nor shall any projection of said building of whatever character be permitted to extend into or encroach upon said space, except that the steps and the platform in front of the main door may be extend over said building line, not to exceed 8 ft.

(b) The Westerly line of all lots, located in Block 1 of said Subdivision shall be 25 ft. from and parallel with the westerly line of Greeg (Gregg) Street, as shown on said Plat, and no building or any part or portion thereof shall at any time be erected or placed upon the space between said building line and the westerly line of Greeg (Gregg) Street, as shown on said Plat; nor shall any projection of said building of whatever character be permitted to extend into or encroach upon said space. Be it understood that Lot 1, located in said Block 1, shall be excepted from this Provision, said Provision being identified as Provision 3-B of the Restrictions on Unit 1 of American Beach, Section 3, a Subdivision of a portion of Tract 3, American Beach, Section 3, according to Plat recorded in Public Records of Nassau County, Florida, in PB 2, Page 64.

(c) Easterly building line of all lots, located in Block 2 of said Subdivision, shall be 25ft. from and parallel with the Easterly line of Greeg (Gregg) Street, as shown on said Plat, and no building or any part or portion thereof shall at any time be erected or placed upon the space of said building line and the Easterly line of Greeg (Gregg) Street, as shown on said Plat, nor shall any projection of said building of whatever character be permitted to extend into or encroach upon said space, except that the steps and the platform in front of the main door may extend over the said building line, not to exceed 8 ft.

(d) The Northerly building line of all lots, located in Block 3 of said Subdivision, shall be 25 ft. from and parallel with the Northerly line of that certain street, fronting said Block, said street intersecting Greeg (Gregg) Street at the South-East corner of Lot 22, Block 2 of said Subdivision.

PARAGRAPH IV

There shall not be erected on any lot, covered by these covenants and restrictions, any building to used for any purpose, other than as a residence.

PARAGRAPH V

There shall not be constructed or suffered to be erected any building on any of the herein restricted lots, to be used as a place for the public sale of liquor or for public gambling.

Further, there shall b e no public sale of liquor or public gambling in any building in said Subdivision, where constructed for said purpose or not.

4

PARAGRAPH VI

No noxious or offensive trade shall be carried on upon any lot, nor shall anything be done thereon, which shall constitute any annoyance or nuisance to the neighborhood.

PARAGRAPH VII

These covenants and restrictions shall run with the land and shall be binding upon the undersigned owner and developer and all grantees of the undersigned and all persons claiming under the undersigned and its grantees from the date hereof, until January 1, 2000, at which time the said covenants and restrictions shall terminate.

PARAGRAPH VIII

If any party or person bound or intended to be bound by these covenants or restrictions or any of them, his heirs or assigns shall violate or attempt to violate any of the said covenants or restrictions before January 1, 2000, any other person or persons owning any other of the said lots shall have the right to prosecute any proceeding at law or in equity, against the person or persons so violating or attempting to violate such covenants or restrictions, either to enjoin such violation or to recover damages therefor.

PARAGRAPH IX

Should any one of the foregoing covenants or restrictions or any part thereof be held by any Court to be invalid, such violation shall not in anywise affect any other covenants or restrictions or part thereof, but the same shall remain in full force and effect.

IN WITNESS WHEREOF, the Afro-American Pension Bureau, Incorporated, has caused these presents to be signed in its name by its Executive Vice President and its Corporate Seal, to be hereto affixed, attested to by its Secretary on this 17th day of August A. D. 1949.

WITNESSES: AFRO-AMERICAN PENSION BUREAU, INC.

_____   By_____
                                                          J. T. BETSCH
                                                          AS ITS EXECUTIVE VICE PRESIDENT
Willie C. McCoy

_____   Attest:_____
                                                          L. D. ERVIN
W. Russell Robinson   AS ITS SECRETARY

5

DEED BOOK 165   **PAGE 336**

STATE OF FLORIDA)

COUNTY OF DUVAL)

Before me personally appeared, J. T. Betsch and L. D. Ervin, to me

known and known to me to be the Executive Vice President and Secretary,

respectively, of the Afro-American Pension Bureau, Incorporated, the

corporation named in the foregoing instrument, and known to me to be the

persons who as such officers of said corporation, executed the same; and

then and there the said J. T. Betsch and the said L. D. Ervin did acknowledge

before me that said instrument is the free act and deed of said

corporation by them respectively executed as such officers for the

purposes therein expressed; that the seal thereunto attached is the

corporate seal by them ikn like capacity affixed; all under authority in

them duly vested by the Board of Directors of said corporation.

WITNESS my hand and official seal this 17th day of August 1949.

Willie C McCoy

Notary Public in and for the County

and State Aforesaid. My Commission expires: Nov. 3, 1950

Register No 35669

Filed and Recorded in the Public Records of Nassau County, Florida in Deed

6

Book No 165 on page 331-336 This 19th day of August A. D., 1949 at 9

o'clock A. M.

Record Verified by T W Broun Clerk Circuit Court

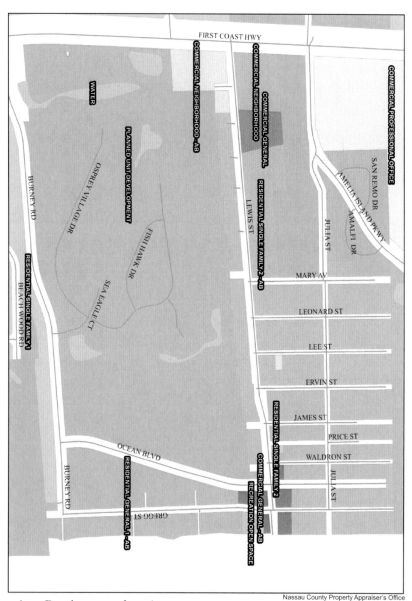

Nassau County Property Appraiser's Office

American Beach area and zoning map.

American Beach, by description, is a platted subdivision identified by block and lot numbers. It is located on the southern unincorporated area of Amelia Island.

Zoning Code: CN-Commercial Neighborhood, RG1- Residential Geaneral, RS2- Residential Single Family, CG- Commercial General, CPO-Commercial Professional Office, PUD-Planned Unit Development.

Property Owners Listing

Listed on the following pages are names, including lot descriptions, of property owners whom I communicated with during my early years of administration as president of the community association.

Over the years, some properties have changed hands to buyers outside the family tree. Yet, other properties have been passed on to relatives or descendants due to loss of family members or for various other reasons.

In 2010, an overwhelmingly number of properties remain under original ownership. All names appear as they are listed on the official roster of record.

Owner/Name	Block & Lot Number
Adams, Henry Lee Jr. & Bernice E.	Block 6, Lot 44
Adams, William H. III & Edna P.	Block 13, Lot 6
Alexander, Andrew Will & Brenda	Block 16, Lot 10
Allen, Leslie E.	Block 6, Lot 42
Allen, Puleston D. & Louise	Block 11, Lot 9
Allen R K	Block 14, Lot 4
Arline, John & James W. & Ella R. Wilson	Block 13, Lot 14
Ashe, Charles	Block 13, Lots 8 & 9
Aveilhe, Elmore T. & Maude	Block 16, Lot 16
Baker, Oliver & Evelena	Block 14, Lot 3
Barnes, Edward U. & Evelyn D.	Block 4, Lot 27
Barnett, M H SR. & Pearl C.	Block 12, Lot 7
Baugh, Rubye E. Estate	Block 11, Lot 11
Beazley, Ronald & Dixon, Gary	Block 1, Lot 7
Bell, Franklin D R & Johnnie J.	Block 17, Lot 15
Boddie, Vivian Moore	Block 16, Lots 7 & 8
Bonner, Ruth S.	Block 10, Lot 81
Braddock, Ronald D & Donald G & Dale P	Block 1, Lot 2
Bridgewater, Richard & Laura V.	Block 15, Lots 3 & 4
Broadway, William L/E Broadway Lottie Mae	Block 4, Lot 26
Brown, Elaine H. Trustee	Block 1, Lots 3 & 4
Brown, Margaret H.	Block 2, Lot 15
Brown, Mary Lawson	Block 7, Lot 49
Burney, I H & Miriam	Block 5, Lot 34
Bush, Comilla & Griffian, Valerie & Jones Eric F. & Quinton A.& Bush Michael D. IV & Jones G L	Block 12, Lots 15 & 16
Bush, Comilla & Griffian Valerie & Jones Eric F. & Quinton A.& Bush Michael D. IV & Jones G L	Block 2, Lot 22
Bush, Comilla E	Block 12, Lot 1
Byrd, James Jr. & Vivian E.	Block 9, Lot 71
Calhoun, Edna Mae	Block 5, Lot 38
Calhoun, Jerome & Gwendolyn B	Block 1, Lot 5

Calhoun, John R.& Frances L.	Block 8, Lot 1
Calhoun, John R.& Frances L.	Block 8, Lot 2
Calhoun, John R.& Frances L.	Block 8, Lot 3
Calhoun, John R.& Frances L.	Block 8, Lot 4
Catron, James B. & Cheryl B.	Block 1, Lot 16
Champ, Thomas & Cheryl	Block 15, Lot 9
Chatman, Jacob L Rev.	Block 11, Lot 8
Childs, Azzie Lee	Block 5, Lot 36
Coleman, Larry J. & Jacquelyn L	Block 10, Lots 3 & 4
Cooper, Leazer Grace	Block 15, Lot 15
Cooper, Leazer Grace	Block 15, Lot 16
Cowart, Ashley & Johnnie	Block 13, Lot 16
Cromer, Adam & Evetta & Dorsey L. Hayes	Block 14, Lot
Davis, Barbara Mungin & Casen Paulette Mungin	
& Mungin Don	Block 14, Lot 8
Davis, Cora & Katie	Block 17, Lot 18
Davis, Granderson	Block 12, Lot 9
Davis, Johnny L. & Cassie J.	Block11, Lot 5
Davis, Johnny L. & Cassie J.	Block11, Lot 6
Davis, Paralee H. & Marie H. Sheehy	Block 10, Lot 79
Davis, Reather M.	Block 17, Lot 12
Davis, William & Margery D.	Block 18, Lot 1
Davis, William & Margery D.	Block 15, Lot 5
Davis, William & Margery D.	Block 15, Lot 6
Davis, William & Margery D.	Block 18, Lot 2
Dawkins Williams W L/E Bruce Sherfield	
& Gladys Wilson	Block 13, Lot 7
Dilliard, Alberta	Block 16, Lot 14
Dollison, Bobby	Block 1, Lot 27
Dollison, Bobby	Block 2, Lot 11
Dukes, Jason & Rodney	Block 13, Lot 15
Edwards, Carl B	Block 11, Lot 1
Edwards, Carl B	Block 11, Lot 2
Edwards, Carl B	Block 11, Lot 3
Edwards, Carl B	Block 11, Lot 4

Edwards, Charles E. & Dorothy S.	Block 17, Lot 2
Edwards, James W.	Block 3, Lot 22
Emory, Eugene K. & Hooks Olivette M.	Block 1, Lot 18
Emory, Eugene K. & Hooks Olivette M.	Block 1, Lot 19
Emory, Eugene K. & Hooks Olivette M.	Block 1, Lot 20
Emory, Eugene K. & Hooks Olivette M.	Block 1, Lot 21
Felder, Carolyn Julia	Block 7, Lots 3 & 4
Fields, Shirley A	Block 18, Lot 8
Fillmore, Beatrice & King Francina C.	Block 11, Lot 10
Flunker, N E Sr. & Johnnie M.	Block 2, Lot 13
Foster, Gladys Delores	Block 18, Lot 6
Foster, John H Jr. & Gladys D	Block 18, Lot 5
Frazier, Vivian & Spencer Christal	Block 12, Lot 3
Frederick, Nathaniel	Block 12, Lot 8
Gadson, Rosella J. L/E	Block 18, Lot 9
Garner, G W & V M	Block 15, Lots 7, 8,11,12
Geiger, Barbara H Trustee	Block 4, Lot 30
Geiger, Barbara H Trustee	Block 4, Lot 31
George, James R Jr. & Marianne Schmitt	Block 1, Lot 26
Gilyard, Erving & Allean	Block 15, Lots 17 & 18
Gilyard, Erving & Allean D	Block 15, Lot 2
Gilyard, Henry C/O Isabella Chatman	Block 2, Lot 7
Gilyard, Henry C/O Isabella Chatman	Block 2, Lot 8
Girardeau, Arnett E. DDS	Block 2, Lot 17
Glover, Ulysses C.	Block 16, Lot 12
Gordie, John M & Oneida	Block 13, Lot 3
Gordie, John M & Oneida E.	Block 13, Lots 1 & 2
Green, George N. & Frances	Block 9, Lots 1 & 2
Green, Theresa & Boykins S.	Block 18, Lot 16
Groomes, Eldrige A. & Michelle R.	Block 10, Lot 77
Guyton, James S. Jr. & Alvergia	Block 16, Lot 13
Guzman, Jessie P.	Block 7, Lot 56
Hall, Ernest B & Athar R.	Block 13, Lot 11
Hall, Ernest B & Athar R.	Block 16, Lot 11
Hansberry,Lauretta & Brenda Onfroy	Block 13, E1/2, Lot 1

Hansberry, Lauretta & Brenda Onfroy | Block 13, E1/2, Lot 2
Harris, Anne Marie | Block 1, Lots 12 & 13
Harris, Tola Jr | Block 4, Lot 32
Hart, Annie Alberta | Block 17, Lot 6
Hartley, Helen H | Block 2, Lot 14
Hayes, John H | Block 2, Lot 21
Henderson, William E & Bernice Henderson, Donald R
Block 7, Lot 53
Hill, John J | Block 10, Lot 80
Hogan, Rosetta C | Block 18, Lots 17 & 18
Holmes, John T | Block 17, Lot 7
Holmes, John T | Block 17, Lots 10 & 11
Hooker, Willie F Sr | Block 2, Lot 10
Iszard, Jerry Jr. & Lois M | Block 1, Lot 14
Iszard, Jerry Jr. & Lois M | Block 1, Lot 15
Jackson, Eddie Mae | Block 16, Lot 16
Jackson, Leroy B & Edna C | Block 14, Lot 5
Jackson, Lougenia C | Block 5, Lot 39
James, Jack Jr | Block 2, Lot 12
James, John J & Katherine | Block 18, Lots 10 & 11
Jenkins, Quality Barbecue of Jacksonville Inc. Block 3, Lot 1
Johnson, Cora D | Block 5, Lot 40
Johnson, Gladys M. & Rega Anderson | Block 5, Lot 3
Johnson, Ishmon & G B | Block 9, Lot 66
Jones, Elizabeth & Intercoastal Mortgage Company
& Associates Inc | Block 1, Lot 6
Jones, Elizabeth Simmons | Block 3, Lot 17
Jones, Thomas & Viola | Block 17, Lot 4
Jones, Thomas Jr. | Block 17, Lot 13
Jordan, Otis M & Shirley Ann | Block 18, Lot 12
Judkins, Robert L & Marion | Block 7, Lot 55
Judkins, Robert L. Sr. & M & Judkins Carmen Block 8, Lot 61
Kelley, Robert J & Emma J | Block 9, Lot 72
Kennedy, Corinne M | Block 12, Lot 10
Kirtsey, Charles J | Block 12, Lot 4

Kowkabany, John B	Block 1, Lot 8
Lanham, Vivian S	Block 12, Lot 2
Lawrie, Dr T L	Block 6, Lot 43
Lawson, Barbara Joyce	Block 8, Lot 63
Leapheart, Gwendolyn & Burwell Gwendolyn L	
	Block 9, Lot 74
Legal Three Inc	Block 10, Lot 75
Leite, Raymond L	Block 1, Lot 28
Lenoir, Jacob E Jr. & Bobby Edward Gibbs	Block 1, Lot 1
Lewis, Ann B	Block 16, Lot 18
Lewis, Ernest Jr.	Block 9, Lot 73
Looney, Faye C.	Block 14, Lot 7
Lucas, William N & Dorothy	Block 2, Lot 20
Lunsford, Walter T & Elizabeth	Block 2, Lot 11
Mahon, Lacy Jr. & Nancy N.	Block 1, Lot 23
Marshall, James L Jr. Janie	Block 17, Lot 3
McCall, Dorothy L Robinson	Block 16, Lot 15
McClenton, Sam Sr. & Ethel P	Block 14, Lot 10
McCloud, Eddie & Zyra	Block 17, Lot 1
McCray, Nathaniel H & Billie C	Block 8, Lot 64
McCully, James G Trustee of Coastal GA Radiology Trust	
	Block 1, Lot 8
Mcintosh, O W	Block 17, Lot 9
Mcintosh, O W	Block 1, Lot 25
Meares, Isaac J	Block 2, Lot 13
Merlini, Joseph C Jr.	Block 12, Lot 2
Miller, Bobbie-Sue B	Block 2, Lots 14 & 15
Mitchell, Lennie	Block 15, Lot 10
Mitchell, Mary Barnett	Block 10, Lot 82
Mitchell, Sollie & M B	Block 4, Lot 2
Mitchell, Sollie & Mary B	Block 4, Lot 1
Molloy, George C & Elsie P	Block 12, Lot 11
Montgomery, Arthur & Mattye	Block 2, Lot 19
Montgomery, Barbara	Block 13, Lot 18
Moore, Allan T Jr.	Block 8, Lot 59

Moore, Alpha H L/E Allan T Jr. & Lionel Moore

	Block 8, Lot 58
Morgan, Emma & Frank	Block 2, Lot 4
Morgan, Emma & Frank	Block 2, Lot 5
Morgan, Emma & Frank	Block 3, Lot 23
Morgan, Frank & Emma	Block 4, Lot 24
Morgan, Frank & Emma	Block 2, Lot 4
Morgan, Frank & Emma H.	Block 2, Lot 10
Morgan, Frank & Emma H.	Block 2, Lot 1
Morgan, Frank & Emma H.	Block 2, Lot 2
Morgan, Frank & Emma H.	Block 2, Lot 3
Morgan, Frank Jr. Trustee	Block 3, Lot 18
Morris, L E Est. & Mcintosh Lorraine	Block 11, Lots 4 & 15
Morris, William A	Block 14, Lot 12
Muldrow ,Oliver R & B S	Block 12, Lot 6
Myers, Annette M	Block 11, Lots 1,2,3,16,17 & 18
Myers, Jeraldine & Ruth Waters	Block 2, Lot 9
Nairn, George B & Sara G	Block 13, Lot 1
Nairn, George B & Sara G	Block 13, Lot 2
Nassau, Country	Block 14, Lots 13 & 14
Nelson, Clarence	Block 4, Lot 29
Nelson, Tony D	Block 2, Lot 12
New Century Corp	Block 15, Lot 1
New Century Corp	Block 2, Lot 1
Norman, Edwin J.	Block 12, Lots 3 & 4
Owens, Wilhelmina Rutledge	Block 4, Lot 28
Palmer, Verdell	Block 17, Lot 5
Pan American Bank Trustee	Block 6, Lot 46
Patterson, George E. & Gloria L/E Patterson Jerral W.	
Roland, F & Patterson Kevin L.	Block 17, Lot 5
Perkins, Kimberly & Beverly	Block 5, Lots 1 & 2
Peterson, Albert	Block 11, Lot 13
Peterson, Albert	Block 11, Lot 14
Phelts, Marsha & Lamar Eva Cobb	Block 10, Lot 11

Phelts, Marsha & Lamar Eva Cobb	Block 10, Lot 2
Phelts, Michael & Marsha R.	Block 10, Lot 11
Phillips, Bradley S.& Hickson Alexander J.	Block 1, Lot 6 & 7
Pierce, Pauline W Smith	Block 6, Lot 45
Plummer, Eddie Lue	Block 14, Lot 15 & 16
Pressley, Leonard C & Gloria	Block 6, Lot 12
Pressley, Leonard C & Gloria J	Block 12, Lot 12
Price, Lewis & Carrie	Block 16, Lot 4
Quarterman, Ernest Jr. & Lois	Block 17, Lot 17
Quarterman, Lois Bradley	Block 18, Lot 14
Quarterman, Lois Bradley	Block 18, Lot 15
Reynolds, Charles M Jr.	Block 13, Lot 17
Richardson, Clara	Block 13, Lot 13
Richardson, Harry V.	Block 7, Lot 52
Robinson, Edward H & V W	Block 12, Lot 7
Robinson, Franklin	Block 4, Lot 3
Robinson, Franklin	Block 4, Lot 4
Robinson, James A. & Joyce E.	Block 16, Lot 9
Robinson, Kathryn P.	Block 2, Lot 18
Robinson, Melba B	Block 13, Lot 10
Rooks, Evelyn B.	Block 1, Lot 17
Russell, Nelly Vonne T	Block 16, Lot 5
Sanders, Theresa H & Smith Metro L.	Block 3, Lot 21
Sears, Frank	Block 17, Lot 14
Sellers, Kenneth G & Ruth Owen	Block 1, Lot 11
Sessions, Ben II & Marie G.	Block 8, Lot 60
Sharpley,Victoria E B & Bywaters Jean Leroy Jr.	
	Block 7, Lot 54
Sheffield, Louise E.	Block 6, Lot 4
Shelby, Ronald J & Courtney	Block 18, Lot 13
Shipp, Horace A.	Block 5, Lot 35
Simmons, C E Jr.	Block 7, Lot 51
Simmons, Isaac D & Emma Mae	Block 13, Lot 12
Simmons, Sara	Block 7, Lots 1 & 2
Smith, Barbara L.	Block 1, Lot 24

Smith, C T & Ruth Smith	Block 18, Lot 7
Smith, Ernestine	Block 1, Lot 9
Smith, Frank U	Block 3, Lot 20
Smith, John R & W S Pryce	Block 11, Lot 7
Smith, Johnny T & June M	Block 17, Lot 8
Solomon, David Brooks	Block 18, Lot 3
Solomon, David Brooks	Block 18, Lot 4
Solomon, Grace B & David Brooks	Block 14, Lot 9
Sothen, Richard A. & Bobbie Amos	Block 1, Lot 9
Sothen, Richard A. & Bobbie Amos	Block 1, Lot 10
Stevens, James S & Joella H	Block 1, Lot 4
Steward, Helen J	Block 9, Lot 67
Sugar Bowl Inc	Block 2, Lot 16
Sugar Bowl Inc	Block 1, Lot 1
Sutton, George A Jr.	Block 13, Lot 4
Sutton, Vivian B	Block 13, Lot 3
Symonette, Elizabeth	Block 16, Lot 17
Takacs, Zsolt B & Ruth J.	Block 1, Lot 29
Thomas, John P Jr & Barbara	Block 7, Lot 50
Thomas, Theodore V & Myrtle P.	Block 6, Lot 2

Thompson, Camilla P & Watkins J Bruce & Muriel T.

                                       Block 1, Lot 22

Tyson, Tommie L. & Henry Joseph N.	Block 11, Lot 12
Varner, Dozell & Emma N.	Block 9, Lot 69
Varner, Dozell & Emma N.	Block 9, Lot 70
Von, Winbush Zete E.	Block 3, Lot 19
Walker, Emmett T & Evelyn	Block 2, Lot 16
Waters, Caesar & Ruth L	Block 15, Lot 13
Waters, Ruth L.	Block 14, Lot 11
Watson, William	Block 5, Lot 41
Weathersbee, W J.	Block 1, Lot 2
Weathersbee, William J	Block 1, Lot 3

Wells, Sula G & Christiana H Campbell & Christopher N Hall II

                                       Block 3, Lot 18

Wilkinson, Juanita	Block 15, Lot 14
William, A C	Block 16, Lot 1 2 3
Williams, Annie Lee	Block 5, Lot 33
Williams, Cozetta Rose L Cromer	Block 14, Lot 2
Williams, Earl & Pearl	Block 14, Lots 17 &18
Williams, Estelle C	Block 13, Lot 5
Williams, Harry D & Nora	Block 5, Lot 4
Williams, Lincoln C & P	Block 4, Lot 25
Williams, Lincoln C Sr. & Pearl & Lincoln C Jr.	
	Block 3, Lot 18
Williams, Rudolph	Block 6, Lot 48
Williams, Rudolph	Block 8, Lot 62
Williams, Rudolph	Block 8, Lot 65
Williams, Rudolph V	Block 1, Lot 5
Williams, Solomon (Est)	Block 10, Lot 78
Williams, Wilma Franklin	Block 5, Lot 37
Wilson, Maxcell Sr. & Betty A.	Block 9, Lot 3
Wilson, Maxcell Sr. & Betty A.	Block 9, Lot 4
Wolfe, Henry D.	Block 14, Lot 6
Wynn, Williams A. Jr & E M	Block 6, Lot 1
Youngblood, Sara	Block 6, Lot 47

Property Owners Profile

Through the years and today, American Beach has always consisted of owners and residents, active and retired, from all walks of life. The preceding list includes professional musicians, educators, various artists, lawyers, doctors, judges, historians, governmental workers, business owners, funeral directors, authors, fashion models, realtors, caterers, preachers, evangelists, photographers, landscapers, building contractors, deputy sheriffs, para-professionals and many other citizens who make up the cultural essence of the community.

In 2011, American Beach continues to be an African-American coastal community, owned and operated by African-Americans. American Beach is the only African-American seaside community remaining in the state of Florida, since the days of segregation, when black people could not attend public beaches. By many historians and others, American Beach is proclaimed to be one of a kind as an African-American coastal community in the United States.

Long Live American Beach!

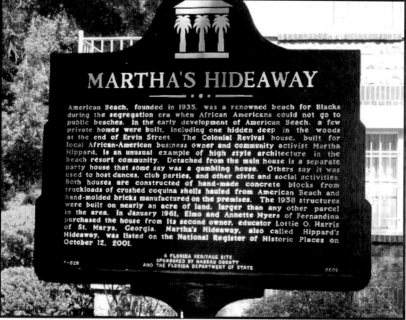

MARTHA'S HIDEAWAY

American Beach, founded in 1935, was a renowned beach for Blacks during the segregation era when African Americans could not go to public beaches. In the early development of American Beach, a few private homes were built, including one hidden deep in the woods at the end of Ervin Street. The Colonial Revival house, built for local African-American business owner and community activist Martha Hippard, is an unusual example of high style architecture in the beach resort community. Detached from the main house is a separate party house that some say was a gambling house. Others say it was used to host dances, club parties, and other civic and social activities. Both houses are constructed of hand-made concrete blocks from truckloads of crushed coquina shells hauled from American Beach and hand-molded bricks manufactured on the premises. The 1938 structures were built on nearly an acre of land, larger than any other parcel in the area. In January 1961, Elmo and Annette Myers of Fernandina purchased the house from its second owner, educator Lottie O. Harris of St. Marys, Georgia. Martha's Hideaway, also called Hippard's Hideaway, was listed on the National Register of Historic Places on October 12, 2001.

A FLORIDA HERITAGE SITE
SPONSORED BY NASSAU COUNTY
AND THE FLORIDA DEPARTMENT OF STATE
7-828   2008

American Beach Community Center and Museum. Building construction completed in 2010. The official grand opening and ribbon cutting was held on March 30, 2010.

Notes

Chapter 1   SUMMERTIME FUN

1. Amy Rosier, "Honey Dripper Memories," *Fernandina Beach News-Leader*, April 19, 2006, A16.

Chapter 2   AMERICAN BEACH SINCE THE 1960s

1. Receipt Number VI, *Charter membership dues*, American Beach, Inc., February 20, 1982.
2. "For the record," *Fernandina Beach News-Leader*, October 31, 1990.
3. Marsha Dean Phelts, *An American Beach for African Americans* (Gainesville: University Press of Florida, 1997) 138.

Chapter 3   AMERICAN BEACH PROPERTY OWNERS'
                  ASSOCIATION, INC. (ABPOA, Inc.)

1. J. L. Laws, "Deputies, crowd clash Sunday," *Fernandina Beach News-Leader*, May 1, 1996, A1, A10.
2. Everett Harpe, "Solutions Sought For Problems at American Beach," *The Nassau Observer*, June 1998.

Chapter 4   NATIONAL REGISTER OF HISTORIC PLACES

1. Michelle Owens, "Reflections On A Heritage/Celebrating Nassau County's Black Heritage," *Fernandina Beach News-Leader*, February 10, 1999, 5.
2. Nassau County Courthouse Records, Covenants and Blanket Restrictions, Unit One of American Beach—Section Three, deed book 165, 331.
3. Kevin Turner, "County Oks historic preservation law," *Fernandina Beach News-Leader*, April 14, 2004, A5.
4. National Register of Historic Places, "Results of Listing In Florida," *Florida Department of State*, Internet 2005.

Chapter 5   WATER AND SEWER INFRASTRUCTURE

1. Turner, "Utility grant sought for American Beach," *Fernandina Beach News-Leader,* September 26, 2003, A1.

2. Ibid.

3. Ibid.

4. Post, Buckley, Schue, and Jernigan(PBS&J), "American Beach Conceptual Water and Sewer Master Plan," prepared for Nassau County (August 28, 2003).

5. Ibid.

6. Nassau County Public Records, advertisement, *Fernandina Beach News-Leader,* November 1990.

7. Michelle Owens, "Property owners learn options for utility service," *Fernandina Beach News-Leader,* November 26, 1997.

8. Alison Trinidad, "Expansion of utilities again delayed-American Beach: Money is problem," *Florida Times-Union/Nassau Neighbors,* June 9, 2004, 2.

9. Ibid.

Chapter 6   THE THREAT OF A COMMUNITY
REDEVELOPMENT AGENCY (CRA)

1. Hope Yen, "Court: Homes can be seized," *Florida Times-Union,* June 24, 2005, A1.

2. Landers-Atkins Planners, Incorporated, *American Beach Overlay Zoning District.* 1997.

3. "Fact Book," *Fernandina Beach News-Leader,* 2005 ed., 14.

4. Nassau County Courthouse Records, *Ordinance No. 2002-63,* established December 16, 2002.

5. Trinidad, "County Oks zone ordinance/American:Change loosens restrictions." *Florida Times-Union/Nassau Neighbors,* December 21, 2002, 1.

6. Landers-Atkins Planners, Incorporated, *American Beach Conceptual Planning Study.* 1995.

7. Turner, "No to CRA on American Beach," *Fernandina Beach*

News-Leader, February 11, 2004, A4.

    8. Ibid.

    9. Trinidad, "American Beach redevelopment plan may not be needed now," *Florida Times-Union/Nassau Neighbors,* December 13, 2003, 3.

Chapter 7   HISTORIC SURVEY OF AMERICAN BEACH FOR THE NATIONAL REGISTER

    1. Joel McEachin, "American Beach Historic Building Survey, Nassau County Florida," prepared for American Beach Property Owners' Association, Incorporated (September 1998) 29.

    2. Ibid.

    3. Ibid.

    4. Ibid., 24.

    Phelts 43-44.

    5. McEachin 31.

    Phelts 44.

    6. McEachin, Appendix A, 46-48.

Chapter 8   MARTHA'S HIDEAWAY

    1. Phelts 49.

    2. Ibid., 50-51.

    3. Ibid., 48.

    Frank Johnson, Jr., oral interview for Martha's Hideaway by Joel McEachin, February 15, 2000.

    4. Gwendolyn Miller, telephone interview, July 13, 2005.

    5. Phelts 52.

    6. "Nassau County NAACP History," *Annual Freedom Fund Banquet Program Booklet,* 2005.

    7. Valerie Boyd, *The Life of Zora Neale Hurston* (New York: Scribner, 2003) 355, 432.

    8. Ibid., 278, 325.

    9. Phelts 66.

10. Rychard S. Cook, II (Miami, Florida), letter to Annette Myers, January 24, 2003.

11. Willie B. Evans, letter to homeowners, May 22, 1967.

12. Gwendolyn Myers Thomas, telephone interview, May 14, 2005.

13. Derek L. Kinner, "A home of long-standing quality/American Beach: No coffins in historic house," *Florida Times-Union/Nassau Neighbors,* August 15, 2001, 1.

Chapter 9   AMERICAN BEACH - NOW BOXED IN

1. Jane Tanner, "Is Change Coming?" *Florida Trend Magazine,* June 1999, 32.

2. *Property Buyers Guide* (Amelia Island, Florida: Amelia Island Plantation, A Sea Pines Community In North Florida, n.d.) AD72-LR-259-B.

3. McEachin 26.

4. Phelts 21.

5. McEachin 19.

6. Ibid., 26-27.

7. Ivy Bigbee, "American Beach," *Folio Weekly,* April 7, 1992, Vol. 6, No. 1: 27.

8. "Annotated Chronology," *Amelia Island Plantation, Nassau County Florida, Plantation Park Project, n.*d.

9. Howard M. Landers, letter, "Dune and maritime forest will be preserved," *Florida Times-Union,* Jaunary 7, 1996.

10. Ander Crenshaw (Congressman), letter, *United States House of Representatives,* dated May 24, 2004

Glenda S. Jenkins, "It's official: American Beach dune is saved," *Fernandina Beach News-Leader,* October 6, 2004, 1.

11. Trinidad, "Beach set for federal protection/Preserve: Beach was African-American," *Florida Times-Union/Nassau Neighbors,* September 29, 2004, 1-2.

12. Trinidad, "County approves purchase of historic land," *Florida Times-Union/Nassau Neighbors,* October 16, 2004, 16.

13. Trinidad, "Beach officially historic," *Florida Times-Union/Nassau Neighbors,* October 9, 2004, 1.

14. Trinidad, September 29, 2004, 1-2.

15. Bob Arndorfer, "Preserving American Beach--It's like home,' *The Gainesville Sun,* May 26, 1996, A1.

Chapter 10   SUNSHINE STATE

1. Liz Flaisig, "Filmmakers on Amelia/A Wonderful Place For A Movie," *Fernandina Beach News-Leader*, March 14, 2001, A1.

Chapter 11   PASSING THE TORCH

1. "American Beach Program," *Presidents' Day, Silver Anniversary Tea,* February 19, 2007.

2. George and Frances Green, telephone interview, August 5, 2010.

Chapter 12   AN AMERICAN BEACH ICON

1 "Kingsley Plantation Ethnohistorical Study," *National Park Service, U. S. Department of the Interior, Southeast Region*, January 2006, Internet.

2. "Obituaries," *Florida Times-Union,* September 8, 2005, B2.

3. Ibid

4. David T. Queen, "Viewpoint: 'Beach Lady' gives hope in the struggle against 'progress,'" *Fernandina Beach News-Leader*, February 18, 2005, A6.

5. MaVynee Betsch, "Commentary," *Fernandina Beach News-Leader*, February 28, 2003.

Bibliographical References

Primary Sources

Carey, Maggie McCollough. Interview. March 18, 2005.

Davis, Curtis B. Interview. April 22, 2005.

Green, George and Frances. Interview. August 5, 2010.

Johnson, Frank, Jr. Interview for Martha's Hideaway by Joel McEachin. February 15, 2000.

Miller, Gwendolyn. Interview. July 13, 2005.

Thomas, Gwendolyn Myers. Interview. May 14, 2005.

Primary Documents and Unpublished Sources

"Annotated Chronology." *Amelia Island Plantation, Nassau County Florida, Plantation Park Project,* n.d.

Cook , II, Rychard S., Miami, Florida. Letter to Annette Myers. January 24, 2003.

Evans, Willie B. Letter to Homeowners. May 22, 1967.

Landers-Atkins Planners, Incorporated. *American Beach Conceptual Planning Study.* Jacksonville, Florida, 1995.

Landers-Atkins Planners, Incorporated. *American Beach Overlay Zoning District.* Jacksonville, Florida, 1997.

McEachin, Joel. "American Beach Historic Building Survey, Nassau County Florida." Prepared for American Beach Property Owners' Association, Inc. September 1998.

Post, Buckley, Schue, and Jernigan (PBS&J). "American Beach Conceptual Water and Sewer Master Plan." Prepared for Nassau County. August 28, 2003.

Receipt Number VI. *Charter membership dues.* American Beach, Inc., February 20, 1982.

Public Documents

Nassau County Courthouse Records. *Ordinance No. 2002-63.* Established December 16, 2002.

Nassau County Courthouse Records. *Covenants and Blanket Restrictions.*

Published Sources and Publications

"American Beach Program." *Presidents' Day, Silver Anniversary Tea,* February 19, 2007.

Arndorfer, Bob. "Preserving American Beach - 'It's like home.'" *The Gainesville Sun,* May 26, 1996.

Bigbee, Ivy. "American Beach." *Folio Weekly,* April 7, 1992, 27.

Betsch, MaVynee. "Commentary." *Fernandina Beach News-Leader,* February 28, 2003.

Boyd, Valerie. *The Life of Zora Neale Hurston.* New York: Scribner, 2003.

Crenshaw, Ander(Congressman). Letter. *United States House of Representatives,* dated May 24, 2004

"Fact Book." *Fernandina Beach News-Leader,* 2005 ed., 14.

Flaisig, Liz. "Filmmakers on Amelia/A Wonderful Place For A Movie." *Fernandina Beach News-Leader,* March 14, 2001.

"For the record." *Fernandina Beach News-Leader,* October 31, 1990.

Harpe, Everett. "Solutions Sought For Problems at American Beach." *The Nassau Observer,* June 1998.

Jenkins, Glenda S. "It's official: American Beach dune is saved." *Fernandina Beach News-Leader,* October 6, 2004.

"Kingsley Plantation Ethnohistorical Study." *National Park Service, U. S. Department of the Interior, Southeast Region,* January 2006, Internet.

Kinner, Derek L. "A home of long-standing quality/American Beach: No coffins in historic house." *Florida Times-Union/ Nassau Neighbors,* August 15, 2001.

Landers, Howard M. Letter. "Dune and maritime forest will be preserved." *Florida Times-Union,* January 7, 1996.

Laws, J. L. "Deputies, crowd clash Sunday." *Fernandina Beach News-Leader,* May 1, 1996.

"Nassau County NAACP History." *Annual Freedom Fund Banquet Program Booklet,* 2005.

Nassau County Public Records. Advertisement. *Fernandina Beach News-Leader,* November 1990.

National Register of Historic Places. "Results of Listing In Florida." *Florida Department of State,* Internet 2005.

"Obituaries." *Fernandina Beach News-Leader,* September 8, 2005.

Owens, Michelle. "Property owners learn options for utility service." *Fernandina Beach News-Leader,* November 26, 1997.

_____."Reflections On A Heritage/Nassau County has a rich black history." *Fernandina Beach News-Leader,* February 10, 1999.

Phelts, Marsha Dean. *An American Beach for African Americans.* Gainesville: University Press of Florida, 1997.

Property Buyers Guide. Amelia Island, Florida: Amelia Island Plantation, A Sea Pines Community In North Florida, n.d.

Queen, David T. "Viewpoint: 'Beach Lady' gives hope in the struggle against 'progress.'" *Fernandina Beach News-Leader,* February 18, 2005.

Rosier, Amy. "Honey Dripper Memories." *Fernandina Beach News-Leader,* April 19, 2006.

Tanner, Jane. "Is Change Coming?" *Florida Trend Magazine,* June 1999.

Trinidad, Alison. "American Beach redevelopment plan may not be needed now." *Florida Times-Union/Nassau Neighbors,* December 13, 2003.

_____."Beach officially historic." *Florida Times-Union/Nassau Neighbors,* October 9, 2004.

_____."Beach set for federal Protection/Preserve: Beach was African-American." *Florida Times-Union/Nassau Neighbors,* September 29, 2004.

_____."County approves purchase of historic land." *Florida Times-Union/Nassau Neighbors,* October 16, 2004.

_____."County Oks zone ordinance/American: Change loosens restrictions." *Florida Times-Union/Nassau Neighbors,* December 21, 2002.

_____."Expansion of utilities again delayed-American Beach: Money is problem." *Florida Times-Union/Nassau Neighbors,* June 9, 2004.

Turner, Kevin. "County Oks historic preservation law." *Fernandina Beach News-Leader,* April 14, 2004.

_____."No to CRA on American Beach." *Fernandina Beach News-Leader,* February 11, 2004.

_____."Utility grant sought for American Beach." *Fernandina Beach News-Leader,* September 26, 2003.

Yen, Hope. "Court: Homes can be seized." *Florida Times-Union,* June 24, 2005.

RELATED REFERENCES

Amelia's Secrets
Maggie Carter-de Vries

An historic fiction novel based on a true story of real events, people and places. The dramatic highlight of this fascinating novel is the historic account leading up to the tragic murder and trial of Ferdinand C. Suhrer, which takes place in Fernandina, Florida, in the 1880s.

AuthorHouse/ISBN 978-1-4343-9479-8

The Flying Dutchmen
Andrew B. Suhrer

An entertaining and detailed historic novel. The author's writing gives a factual account of the 107th Regiment of the Ohio Volunteer Infantry of the American Civil War. The novel covers much information about the his great-grandfather Ferdinand C. Suhrer, his time spent in the Union Army of the Civil War and Suhrer's life in Fernandina, Florida, in the 1800s.

AuthorHouse/ISBN 978-1-4343-8630-4

Anna Madgigine Jai Kingsley
Daniel L. Schafer

An African-born slave teenager, Anna became the emancipated wife of Zephaniah Kingsley, Jr., a planter and slave trader from Spanish East Florida. Kingsley was the owner of Kingsley Plantation just south of Amelia Island in Duval County. After her husband's death, a remarkable business woman, Anna owned and operated her own plantation.

University Press of Florida/ISBN 0-8130-2616-4

Tidewater Amelia
Jan H. Johannes
Tidewater Amelia is a great photographic work, of homes and buildings, detailing the history of Nassau County, Florida and surrounding communities.

Lexington Ventures/ISBN 0-9677419-2-0

Yesterday's Reflections II
Jan H. Johannes
This book is more than a picturesque chronology of events detailing our place in the passage of time. It is a passport that takes the reader on a journey through time in Nassau County, Florida and surrounding areas.

Lexington Ventures/ISBN 0-9677419-0-4

The Big Sand Dune and The Beach Lady
Annette McCollough Myers
A true historic picture book story about the history of Florida's only African-American seaside community, the big sand dune named "NaNa," and the widely known "Beach Lady." This, 2010 National Indie Excellence Award winning, multi-purpose book is written for all ages to 100-plus.

High-Pitched Hum Publishing/ISBN 978-1-934666-50-0

75th Anniversary Edition of The American Beach Book of Homes
Marsha Dean Phelts
The American Beach Book of Homes documents historic landmarks, past and present, in the geographical area of the historic American Beach community.

High-Pitched Hum Publishing/ISBN 978-1-934666-71-5

The Author

A 2010 National Indie Excellence Award Winning Author

Annette McCollough Myers is a Fernandina Beach, Florida, native. She is a retired educator, community activist and author. Her career has included teaching in the educational system on various levels, high school guidance counselor, grant writing, consulting, mortuary services, and journalism.

Annette earned her Bachelor of Science degree from Florida Agricultural and Mechanical University in Tallahassee, Florida, Master of Science degree from Indiana State University in Terre Haute, Indiana, and her Educational Specialist degree from Nova University in Fort Lauderdale, Florida.

She is the mother of son Donald (Dedria) Myers, and foster daughter, Alria Wilson Mundy. In October 2010, a proud grandmother welcomed her first grandchild, Delaney Ann Myers, into the McCollough-Myers ancestry.

When time permits, the author travels between Fernandina Beach, Miami, Savannah, Georgia, and Gary, Indiana.

To order American Beach books by the author, see websites on page 103 or visit your favorite bookstore.